THE ARK OF SALVATION

THE ARK OF SALVATION

A Young Adult's Guide to the Orthodox Church

The Fathers of Saint Edward Brotherhood

Second Edition 2020

ISBN 978-0-947935-05-4

Published by King Edward Orthodox Trust
Saint Cyprian's Avenue
Brookwood
SURREY
GU24 0BL
www.saintedwardbrotherhood.org

ACKNOWLEDGMENTS

Bishop Ambrose of Methone
Jon Davies, Knaphill Print
Sofia Popova

PHOTO CREDITS

p. 112. Electron cryo-microscopy of Human Papillomavirus Type 16 capsid Image from the RCSB PDB (rcsb.org) of PDB ID 3J6R (Giovanni Cardone, Adam L. Moyer, Naiqian Cheng, Cynthia D. Thompson, Israel Dvoretzky, Douglas R. Lowy, John T. Schiller, Alasdair C. Steven, Christopher B. Buck, Benes L. Trus) Maturation of the Human Papillomavirus 16 Capsid *mBio* Aug 2014, 5 (4) e01104-14

p.130. Agouti Mice by Randy Jirtle and Dana Dolinoy – emailed by author. Kermode Bear iStock.com/jonmccormackphoto

CONTENTS

Jesus the Great Shepherd of the Sheep

The verse on the open Gospel Book is: 'I am the Good Shepherd and I lay down My Life for the sheep.' The scenes in the four corners (clockwise from bottom left) illustrate the following Gospel verses:

I know My sheep and am known of Mine.

The Son of Man is come to seek and save the lost.

When He hath found it, He layeth it on His shoulders, rejoicing.

Then there will be joy in heaven.

GOD

We'll begin by discussing what the Orthodox Church teaches about God because, as St. John Climacus says, it's best to start with God when writing to the servants of God.

Unlike in some non-Orthodox religions, in Orthodoxy we don't imagine what God wants or likes; we have to stick to what the Church teaches about God. No one in this world will ever know everything about God because this is impossible. Only by living an Orthodox life can we strengthen our faith in God and feel, in some small part, God's love for us.

THE TRINITY

We believe in one God in Trinity: Father, Son and Holy Spirit. Each Person is completely God, but the Persons differ in their relationship to each other.

It's hard to describe the idea of the Trinity in words. Imagine three lighted candles held close together. The three flames merge into one, but this single flame is formed from the flames of three candles.

The relationships between the Persons that have been revealed to us are: the Father begets, the Son is begotten and the Holy Spirit proceeds. The word 'begotten' describes the relationship between a son and his father. God the Holy Spirit is not begotten but proceeds from the Father.

God the Son is begotten of the Father before time, but without a mother. The Son of God is often called the Word of God. The Gospel of St. John starts with the following verse: 'In the beginning was the Word, and the Word was with God, and the Word was God.'

ESSENCE AND ENERGIES

God is unknowable and unapproachable in His essence or 'God-ness'. However, it's possible to know God through the energies that come from God. These energies are not small pieces of God or little packets of holiness that God makes for us; these energies are God and are uncreated because God is uncreated. These uncreated energies of God are called grace.

Consider the sun, it shines and we feel and see its rays. These rays cannot be small suns because however sunny it is, the sun doesn't become less hot or less bright. The 'sun' we feel on our skin is its energy. We're partaking of the energy of the sun but we aren't feeling the sun itself in its essence or 'sun-ness'. If we felt even 1% of the sun's essence we would be destroyed by the heat! So we can say that the sun's essence is unapproachable, but its energies are approachable.

The comparison we made with the sun is OK but not quite exact. God's energies are not 'God-waves' – they are God. However, they are not the essence of God. In contrast, the energy that comes from the sun is not 'sun', but it is the light and energy of the sun.

God's energies are not limited by time or space. God acts through His energies in order to support His creation. Father George of the Holy Mountain explains this:

> With His uncreated energies, God created the world and continues to create it. He gives substance and being to our world with His creative energies. He is ever present in nature and provides for the world through His preserving energies. He illuminates man with His illumining energies. He sanctifies him with His sanctifying energies. Lastly, He deifies him through His deifying energies.[*]

St. Athanasius of Alexandria says that God became man so that He might make man god. God is unknowable and unapproachable in His essence, but we can become gods through His uncreated energies. The aim of the Christian life is to become gods by grace which is called deification.

---

[*] Archimandrite George, *Deification As The Purpose Of Man's Life* (Mt. Athos: Monastery of Gregoriou, 2001) p.31

CREATION

God existed before time began. More correctly speaking, God existed before the ages. The word 'ages' describes an endless period that is so long it doesn't even have time! We believe that God existed before the ages because He also created time. God is the Creator of all things but no one created God.

God created the universe from nothing and brought it into being from non-being. Before the creation of the world, the devil, who is also called Satan, fell from Heaven. The cause of this fall was pride; he wanted to be as powerful as God. For this sin of pride, Satan and those angels with him were cast out of Heaven. These angels are called demons and they are, as St. Paul says, 'the rulers of the darkness of this world.'

God created the first man, Adam, in His image. God also fashioned a woman as his companion whom Adam called Eve. Adam and Eve lived in Paradise (also called the Garden of Eden), but they lived there in a different way to how we live on earth now. Like little children they weren't ashamed of their nakedness.

Paradise is a real place but also a spiritual place. So the fruit is real fruit, the water is real water, but the fruit and water are somehow different to what they're like on earth.

Adam, however, wasn't fully grown spiritually, which is why God gave him the commandment not to eat fruit from the 'tree of the knowledge of good and evil.' Unfortunately, the devil, taking the form of a serpent, tempted Eve and she persuaded Adam to eat of the fruit. As a result of this fall into sin, Adam and Eve were thrown out of Paradise.

INCARNATION

The word 'incarnation' means 'putting on flesh'. Even though He existed from before the ages, the Son of God was born in Bethlehem. He became incarnate and was revealed to the world as Jesus Christ. The word Christ means 'anointed one'.

In the Old Testament, kings and priests were anointed with special oil called chrism. In the case of Christ, His human nature is anointed by God.

Christ came to earth and joined God and man perfectly together in Himself. He became man exactly like us, except without sin. He is perfect God and perfect man; these two natures are joined perfectly together but not mixed.

By becoming incarnate, Christ united His divine nature with our human nature and raised it even higher than the angels. He re-opened the path to union with God that Adam had closed by his disobedience. It is for this reason that Christ is called the Second Adam.

Christ's birth in Bethlehem was different from any other human birth because the Virgin Mary was a virgin before, during and after childbirth. For this reason we refer to her as the Ever-Virgin Mary.

She is also called *Theotokos* which is a Greek word meaning 'birthgiver of God' and often translated as simply 'Mother of God'. She is called this because she carried God in her womb and gave birth to Him.

Some people cannot understand how God can have a mother. However, if we believe that Christ is perfect God and perfect man, then His mother must be called Theotokos because she gave birth to God. If she isn't the Mother of God, then Christ is not truly God.

We confess our belief in the Trinity and the incarnation when we make the sign of the Cross (*right*). The thumb, index and middle finger held together represent the Trinity, and the ring and little finger folded down represent the two natures of Christ: God and man.

So, in Christ there are two births! The Son of God was begotten of the Father before the ages without mother and Christ was born in Bethlehem from a mother without father. These two births are mysterious and defy human explanation – don't try and think about it too much!

CHRIST THE SAVIOUR

The name Jesus means 'Saviour' or 'He who saves'. Christ became man to save man. He did this by sacrificing Himself on the Cross for the sins of the world.

We have heard of the Old Testament Passover when the Hebrews were slaves of Pharaoh. To free the Hebrews, God sent various plagues on the Egyptians, the last of which was the killing of all the firstborn of Egypt. God commanded the Hebrews to sacrifice a lamb and paint its blood on the door posts of their houses so that the angel of God might 'pass over' them and their first born be saved.

Christ is our Passover. This is why He is called the Lamb of God that takes away the sins of the world. The word 'Pascha' actually comes from the Hebrew word meaning 'passover'. Christ is our Passover because He has saved us from death by His death on the Cross. This is why we sing at Pascha: 'Christ is risen from the dead, by death hath He trampled down death and on those in the graves hath He bestowed life.'

THE SECOND COMING OF CHRIST

When Christ comes again to earth the dead will hear His voice and rise from the graves. The whole world will be renewed as St. Symeon the New Theologian explains: 'The earthly creation which is visible and accessible to the senses will be transformed and join with the heavenly invisible world that is above the senses.'

Christ will come to earth to judge the living and the dead. This is called the Final or Last Judgement. After the Judgement, sinners will be sent to a place of punishment called Hell or Gehenna, but the righteous will live eternally with Christ in Heaven.

God didn't create Hell because everything that God creates is good. We have made Hell for ourselves. This torment is the separation from God that we have chosen. Think about the sun - the sun's light shines on everyone but we feel it differently. For some it is a pleasure but that same light can burn others. God loves sinners because He is Love, but for the sinners in Hell this love will be a torment.

FREQUENTLY ASKED QUESTIONS

Can you explain about Paradise, Heaven, Hades and Hell?

Before Christ's death on the Cross, everyone that died on earth went to place called Hades, but they didn't suffer there. Hades was like a waiting room. After His death, Christ descended with His soul into Hades and preached His Gospel there.

Because of Christ's resurrection, the souls of the righteous are no longer sent to Hades but to Paradise. Christ said to the thief on the Cross, 'Today thou shalt be with Me in Paradise.' The souls of the righteous receive a foretaste of Heaven in Paradise. Hades, meanwhile, is no longer just a waiting room. The souls of sinners there receive a foretaste of Hell.

Some writers use the word 'heaven' instead of 'paradise'. This isn't a problem. Heaven, Paradise and the Kingdom of God are all words that describe eternal life with Christ.

Why are we guilty of Adam's sin?

We aren't guilty, we just inherit certain things as a result of his sin (often called original sin). Everyone gets ill, we will all eventually die, and our bodies will decompose in the earth. We also inherit from Adam a tendency towards sin. We find it easier to choose evil over good.

THE SOUL

Our soul gives us life. When the heart beats, it's the soul that gives it the power to do so. In man, the word soul has another meaning; it means the spiritual part of our existence. In Christianity, when we talk about the soul we are not referring to its power of giving life, but to this spiritual part of us that we call the inner man. When we eat or drink we are feeding the outer man. When we fast, pray and receive Holy Communion we are purifying and feeding the inner man: our soul.

The soul is not restricted to any one part of the body, but is spread throughout the body with its centre in the heart. This may seem difficult to understand especially as we are taught at school that the heart is just a pump. It obviously isn't, but we will talk about this later.

The Church does not accept the idea of souls floating around somewhere waiting for a body (reincarnation). St. Anastasius of Sinai says that 'neither does the body exist before the soul, nor does the soul exist before the body.'

Only God is without beginning; He existed before the ages. Our souls, on the other hand, have a beginning because they are created by God. Our souls are also immortal; when our body dies our soul lives on. However our souls aren't immortal by nature, but only because God has made them this way.

THE SOULS OF THE DEPARTED

Christ destroyed death by His death on the Cross, so death is now just sleep. This is why in Church services we refer to those people who have died as 'fallen asleep' or 'departed'.

When we die we will be judged and receive a foretaste of Hell or Heaven. This judgment is not final though. Only at the Second Coming of Christ will everyone be judged finally and receive the eternal reward for their deeds on earth.

HOLY MARTYR VARUS

Save, O Master Christ, save, have mercy, and grant rest unto the souls of Thy people that have finished their life in faith with trembling, in whatsoever place and every land, and deliver them from Gehenna and the bitterness of torments, that we may praise Thee unto all the ages.

From the Pentecostarion

The souls of the departed are helped by our prayers in which we ask God to have mercy on them. One way we help those who have fallen asleep is by having memorial services said for them. A memorial service is a bit like a small funeral service. They are normally held on the fortieth day after someone has fallen asleep, and every year on the anniversary of their repose and on their nameday.

We can't hold memorial services for the non-Orthodox, but we can pray for them in our private prayers. The Martyr Varus, in particular, intercedes for those who have died outside the Orthodox Church. We should give money to charity in their memory too.

KOLYVA

We remember and honour our departed relatives by making *kolyva*. The tradition of blessing kolyva (pronounced kol-ee-va) dates back to the fourth century when the Emperor Julian the Apostate ordered that food in the markets be sprinkled with the blood of animals sacrificed to idols. By doing this he hoped to break the morale of the Christians. Through God's mercy, the Great Martyr Theodore appeared to the bishop in a vision and told him to order the Christians to boil wheat (called kolyva) as a replacement for the food in the markets.

Kolyva Recipe

- Arrange a time with the priest for the memorial service.
- On the day before, boil some whole wheat grain until it's soft. 500g of wheat will make enough kolyva for about 30 people.
- Drain the wheat and dry it between paper towels overnight.
- On the next day, mix the wheat with dried fruits, chopped nuts, glacé cherries, pomegranate seeds etc.
- Put the wheat and fruits in a bowl. Sprinkle a little crushed biscuit on the wheat to absorb any moisture.

- Sieve icing sugar onto the wheat to make a layer about 1cm thick. Press the sugar down gently and then decorate the top with nuts or glacé cherries in the form of a cross.
- At church, push a candle into the centre of the kolyva.

FREQUENTLY ASKED QUESTIONS

Do animals have souls?

Anything that shares in the life-giving energies of God has a soul. St. Maximus the Confessor says:

> Lower creatures such as plants have life and their souls have the power of nourishment and growth. The souls of animals also have the power of imagination and instinct. The souls of men have all these powers as well as the powers of intelligence and thought. *

It's obvious that animals have souls because they show emotion. For example, they get angry and they show love. There are many true stories of wild animals befriending people who have looked after them – the famous YouTube video of Christian the Lion is just one example.

Animals, however, don't have rational souls. This means that they're not responsible for their actions. When a lion kills someone it's acting on instinct – it hasn't done anything wrong. Also, the souls of animals aren't immortal. When an animal dies, its soul dies too.

Do ghosts exist?

After death, souls do not float about the earth from place to place. The souls of the departed are consigned to either Paradise or Hades according to the deeds that they have committed in their life. Ghosts can appear to people, but these ghosts are not the souls of the dead; they're demons that have taken on the appearance of people to deceive us.

---

* St. Nikodimos Hagiorites, St. Makarios, *The Philokalia Vol. 2* trans. G.E.H. Palmer, P. Sherrard, K. Ware (London: Faber & Faber, 1981), p.88

THE ORTHODOX CHURCH

The Church is the Body of Christ. The Head of the Church is Christ and we are members of His Body.* All living and departed Orthodox Christians, the saints and the angels are members of this Body. The Church is also often called a vine; Christ is the stem and we are the branches that receive their food and strength from Him.

The Church began with the creation of the angels. All the holy men and women of the Old Testament were members of the spiritual Church. When the Holy Spirit came down in the form of tongues of fire on Pentecost, the apostles became members of the physical Church.

Orthodox bishops are the successors of the apostles. Our bishops are also called hierarchs which is a Greek word meaning 'high priest' or 'leader in holy things'. Each bishop is in charge of a group of churches called a diocese.

The bishop is responsible for everything in his diocese, but he's not a ruler or a judge. He leads us like a shepherd because he is an icon of Christ the Good Shepherd. When we honour and reverence our bishop, we honour Christ through him.

The Orthodox Church is traditional. We don't change any part of the faith that we have received from the Church Fathers. The Orthodox Church is not a museum though. On the contrary, the Church is a living, breathing organism that is constantly being renewed by the Holy Spirit. The Church is always up to date!

HISTORY OF THE CHURCH

Decisions regarding the Church as a whole are taken by all the bishops together when they meet in a Council (also called a Synod). The most important councils are the seven Ecumenical Councils, the last of which was held in AD 787. The word 'Ecumenical' comes from the Greek for 'inhabited

---

* The word 'member' in this sense means a body part.

world' because in these councils bishops came from all over the world to confirm the Orthodox Faith.

The Ecumenical Councils were an Orthodox response to various new ideas which we call heresies. A heresy is any religious teaching that is different to what the Orthodox Church teaches.

Many non-Orthodox Christians believe in one of these ancient heresies without even realising it. The three most common are:

Arianism. The leader of Arianism was a priest called Arius who lived in Alexandria in the fourth century. He taught that Christ is the Son of God, but not actually God. He did not believe in the Trinity.

Nestorianism. Nestorius rejected the Orthodox teaching that the two natures in Christ are joined together in One Person without confusion or division. He suggested that the divine nature passes through the human nature like water through a pipe. He refused to call the Virgin Mary 'Theotokos' but only 'Christotokos' (the Mother of Christ).

Iconoclasm. Iconoclasm is a Greek word that means 'icon breaking'. The iconoclasts (the icon breakers) believed that it was wrong to paint icons of God and the saints because the making of idols was forbidden in the Old Testament. The iconoclasts were a very powerful faction and persecuted Orthodox Christians.

IMPORTANT DATES IN CHURCH HISTORY

49 – Council of Jerusalem chaired by the Apostle James

313 – Emperor Constantine the Great ends the persecution of Christians in the Roman Empire.

325 – 1st Ecumenical Council condemns Arianism

431– 3rd Ecumenical Council condemns Nestorianism

787 – 7th Ecumenical Council confirms the veneration of icons.

988 – Conversion of Russia begins.

1054 – Roman Church and Orthodox Church officially separate.

1066 – Norman Conquest of Britain. Orthodox bishops are replaced with those loyal to Rome.

1204 – Sack of Constantinople by the Crusaders.

1453 – Turks conquer Constantinople.

1918 – Martyrdom of the Russian Royal Family by the Communists.

1924 – New Calendar introduced by some Orthodox Churches.

THE CHURCH CALENDAR

Traditional Orthodox Churches use the Julian or 'Old' Calendar. Every country used to use this calendar (it was used in England until 1752), but now they use the Gregorian Calendar which is thirteen days ahead of the Julian. In other words, when we celebrate Christmas on 25 December, the rest of the world considers that day to be 7 January.

The dates of all our Church feasts are calculated according to the Old Calendar but some of these feasts are fixed and some are on different dates every year.

Paschal Calendar. Pascha always falls on a Sunday but the date is different every year. This is because the timing of the feast of Pascha takes into account various factors including the phases of the moon and the timing of the Jewish Passover.

Fixed Calendar. Christmas Day is on 25 December every year so it can fall on any day of the week. The feast days of saints are also on this fixed calendar and are always on the same date year after year. It's worth mentioning that we celebrate Christmas on 25 December because this is the day that the Church has chosen. It's not 'Christ's birthday'.

The Inside of an Orthodox Church

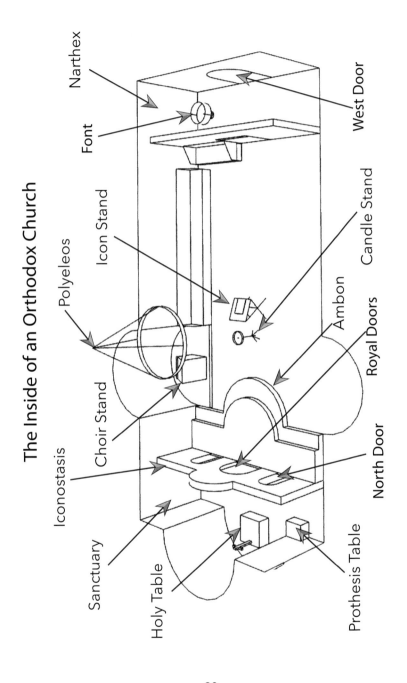

Narthex

Font

West Door

Polyeleos

Icon Stand

Candle Stand

Ambon

Royal Doors

Iconostasis

Choir Stand

North Door

Sanctuary

Holy Table

Prothesis Table

THE MYSTERIES

God sends forth His grace upon everyone in the world, but it's only within the Orthodox Church that we can receive this grace in full. Only within Orthodoxy can we become gods by grace.

Within the Church we partake of the grace of God through the mysteries. In a mystery, physical matter is transformed by the grace of the Holy Spirit. For example, in the Mystery of Baptism, the water grants us forgiveness of sins and we are reborn in it. In the Mystery of the Eucharist, the bread and wine offered becomes the Body and Blood of Christ.

St. John Chrysostom explains that 'in a mystery, what we believe is not the same as what we see, but we see one thing and believe another.'

The seven most important mysteries of the Church are:

- Baptism
- Chrismation
- The Eucharist
- Repentance (Confession)
- Ordination
- Marriage
- Holy Unction

We will discuss the Mysteries of the Eucharist, Repentance and Marriage in separate chapters. It's not possible to rank the mysteries in order of importance, but the Mystery of Baptism is the first one we participate in.

Baptism

Our life in the Church starts at our baptism when we are born again through water and the Holy Spirit. We die in the water and rise out of it a new creation, risen with Christ. We put on Christ and become members of the Orthodox Church.

The word baptism means 'dipping' or 'immersion' so we always immerse the person in the water rather than sprinkling water over them. The person being baptized is immersed three times in the water and at the same time the priest says 'The servant of God [Name] is baptized in the Name of the Father, Amen. And of the Son, Amen. And of the Holy Spirit, Amen.'

Any Orthodox Christian can baptize a baby who is in danger of death. If we don't have enough water to immerse properly we can pour or sprinkle water over the baby instead whilst saying the words that the priest says above.

Chrismation

In the Mystery of Chrismation we receive the gift of the Holy Spirit. We are anointed by the priest with special oil called chrism as the priest says 'the seal of the gift of the Holy Spirit.'

In earlier times, important documents were sealed with wax and then a stamp of the writer was pressed into the hot wax to make a secure mark of ownership. The chrism is a physical sign of the Holy Spirit coming down upon us. Chrismation makes us sealed members of Christ's Church.

Ordination

Men receive the grace to become priests in the Mystery of Ordination. Deacons are ordained too. They assist the priests in the services. Although Orthodox Bishops are monks, priests and deacons can be married. They must, however, marry before they're ordained. They can't marry afterwards.

In Scripture and Tradition we hear of women prophets, deaconesses and martyrs, but never women priests or bishops. Why is this? The priest is a man because Christ became man. The priest is an icon of Christ.

However, it's not the priest who causes the bread and wine to become Christ's Body and Blood: this is done by Christ Himself. St. John Chrysostom explains: 'The priest stands before us, doing what Christ did and speaking the words that He spoke; but the power and grace are from God.'

Even though women are not ordained priests, the goal of every Orthodox Christian is the same. We must struggle to inherit the Kingdom of Heaven. St. Basil the Great says that 'the virtue of man and woman is the same; creation is equally honoured in both, therefore there is the same reward for both.'

Holy Unction

In the Mystery of Unction, Orthodox Christians are anointed with a mixture of olive oil and wine. The oil is blessed in a special service usually celebrated on the Wednesday evening of Great Week (the week before Pascha).

Anointing with oil is a very ancient practice. St. James the Apostle tells us: 'Is any sick among you? Let him call for the elders of the Church, and let them pray over him, anointing him with oil in the name of the Lord.' By this anointing, the grace of God is able to heal sickness of the soul and the body.

THE CHURCH SERVICES

The Orthodox Church has a daily cycle of services including an early evening service called Vespers and a morning service called Matins. There's even a service at midnight!

There are special hymns sung on Great Feasts such as Christmas and for the feasts of the Saints. The shortest of these are called Dismissal Hymns or *apolytikia* in Greek. The Dismissal Hymn for Christmas begins: 'Thy Nativity O Christ our God has shined the light of knowledge upon the world...' We can find these Dismissal Hymns in our Prayer Book and we should try to learn the words even if we can't sing very well.

On Sunday we celebrate Christ's Resurrection and there are eight sets of Resurrection hymns in each of the eight tones (a tone is like a musical scale). These hymns are in a book called the *Octoechos* which means 'eight tones' in Greek. We use a different tone each week, and once we have reached Tone Eight we start again the next Sunday with Tone One.

The hymns we sing for the saints are found in a book called the *Menaion*, which comes from the Greek word for 'month'. There are twelve volumes in the Menaion, one for each month.

There are two other important books used by the choir. The *Triodion* contains all the hymns of Great Lent (the fast before Pascha). The *Pentecostarion* contains the hymns sung from Pascha to the week after Pentecost.

Before the Divine Liturgy on feast days we read a short service called the Third Hour, followed by one called the Sixth Hour. The First Hour is read after Matins and the Ninth Hour before Vespers. These are found in the *Horologion* or 'Book of Hours'.

Time was worked out differently in the Roman world. The first hour of the day started at sunrise. The prayers read in the Hours recall events in the Gospels that happened at specific hours of the day:

- Christ was led before Pilate at the first hour (sunrise).
- The Holy Spirit descended on the apostles at the third hour (9 a.m.).
- Christ was nailed to the Cross at the sixth hour (noon).
- Christ died on the Cross at the ninth hour (3 p.m.).

> *O Sovereign Master, God the Father Almighty, O Lord the Only-begotten Son, Jesus Christ, and Thou, O Holy Spirit, one Godhead, one Power, have mercy on me, a sinner; and by the judgments which Thou knowest, save me, Thine unworthy servant; for blessed art Thou unto the ages of ages. Amen.*
>
> *From the Great Horologion*

THE SYMBOL OF FAITH

Our Orthodox faith is summarised in the Symbol of Faith written by the Fathers of the first two Ecumenical Councils. The Symbol of Faith is often called the Creed after the Latin word *credo* meaning 'I believe.'

I believe in One God, the Father Almighty, Maker of heaven and earth, and of all things visible and invisible;

God made the world, both the things we can see (the visible things) and also the things that are invisible such as our souls and the angels. The word 'Almighty' means 'all powerful'. No one can resist the power of God but we also know that God is our Father. He loves us – He loves us so much that 'He gave His only begotten Son, that whoever believes in Him should not perish, but have everlasting life.'

And in one Lord, Jesus Christ, the Son of God, the Only-begotten, begotten of the Father before all ages; Light of Light, true God of true God; begotten not made; being of one essence with the Father; by Whom all things were made;

Christ is called 'Light' because those that follow Him do not walk in darkness, but have the light of life. He is true God of true God because even though He is begotten of the Father He is not inferior to the Father. He is completely God and one in essence with the Father and the Holy Spirit.

Who for us men, and for our salvation, came down from the Heavens, and was incarnate of the Holy Spirit and the Virgin Mary, and became man;

Here we confess our belief in the incarnation. The Son of God came down from the Heavens and became man, but He was not separated from the Father and the Holy Spirit.

And was crucified for us under Pontius Pilate, suffered and was buried;

Christ is dual in nature; He is perfect God and perfect Man. These two natures are joined perfectly together but not mixed. Only Christ's human nature suffered on the Cross; His divine nature was unharmed because God is almighty.

And arose again on the third day according to the Scriptures;

Through His resurrection Christ defeated death and showed that we also will rise again. Christ was crucified and buried on Friday and arose from the dead early on Sunday morning. This is the 'third' day because we count Friday and Sunday too.

And ascended into the Heavens, and sitteth at the right hand of the Father;

Christ ascended into Heaven bodily. By sitting at the right hand of the Father He raised our human nature higher than it ever was before. It is higher now than Adam was before he fell. This is why Christ is called the Second Adam.

And shall come again, with glory, to judge both the living and the dead; Whose Kingdom shall have no end.

Christ's Second Coming will be completely different to His first when He was born in Bethlehem unknown to the world. It will be a solemn, terrible day in which we will receive the rewards for our life on earth.

Christ will come in glory and there will be no need for anyone to tell us that He has arrived – the light and glory will shine from one end of the earth to the other. Those of us who have died will then be judged along with those found living on earth. We must repent and change our lives on earth so that we can give a good answer at the Final Judgement.

And in the Holy Spirit, the Lord, the Giver of Life; Who proceedeth from the Father; Who with the Father and the Son together is worshipped and glorified; Who spake by the prophets;

The Persons of the Godhead are different but One in essence. We worship the Father and the Son together with the Holy Spirit. The prophets were inspired by the Holy Spirit to speak of things that would happen in the future and to reveal hidden mysteries.

In One Holy, Catholic, and Apostolic Church.

One. The Church is one because it is the Body of Christ. We also believe that only in this 'one' Church can we find salvation. The Church isn't divided into branches with each containing a small part of the Church; each Orthodox church building and the people together are the whole Church.

Holy. The Church is holy because it is the Body of Christ. Although we are sinners, by being members of the Church we can be united with Christ. Only within this Holy Church can we partake of the Body and Blood of Christ in the Eucharist.

Catholic. The word catholic means 'universal'. The Church is called catholic because it is known throughout the world and possesses all truth. It is also called catholic because we have a common life in Christ in the Church. We're united together in faith as members of the Body of Christ.

Apostolic. The word apostle means 'someone who is sent'. The Church is called apostolic because Christ was sent by the Father. He is the Father's Apostle as St. Justin the Martyr writes:

> Much has been written to prove that Jesus the Christ is the Son of God and the Father's Apostle. He is the Word Who existed from before the ages, Who appeared sometimes in the form of fire, and sometimes in the likeness of angels; but now, by the will of God, He has become man for the race of man.

The Church is called apostolic because she teaches the same faith as the apostles did. The Church is also apostolic because our bishops are ordained in a continuous line of succession from the apostles.

I confess one baptism for the remission of sins.

Baptism is 'one' because we're only baptized once and because there's only one place where true baptism is found: the Orthodox Church.

I look for the resurrection of the dead, and the life of the age to come. Amen.

We will rise from the grave in the same body in which we lived here on earth. However, this body will no longer be restricted by the laws of nature. Our bodies will be renewed and spiritual – like Christ's body after the resurrection.

When He appeared to the disciples and was touched by the Apostle Thomas, the nail marks in His hands and feet and the hole made by the spear were still there, but His body was no longer bound by nature's laws. We know this because He entered the room whilst the doors were shut.

After the resurrection of the dead, the righteous will inherit the Kingdom of God. This life of the age to come will never end. It is often called 'eternal life' in the church services.

O Unity of Threefold splendour, Who of old broughtest out of non-being the nature of all things visible and invisible, and Who deliverest from all temptations them that faithfully praise Thee as one God, count us worthy of Thy Glory.

From the Pentecostarion

THE BIBLE

The Bible contains all the books of the Old and New Testaments. These books are the sacred writings of Christianity and are called Scripture. The Scriptures weren't written by God, but were written by people inspired by God.

The Old Testament is the Scripture that the Christian Church inherited from the Jews. The New Testament contains the four Gospels, a book called the Acts of the Apostles, the epistles (letters) of the apostles and the Book of Revelation.

A 'testament' is a type of agreement. In the Old Testament, we hear about the agreement between God and the Hebrews in which they promised to obey God's Law as His chosen people. The word 'testament' also has the meaning of 'witness'. The writings of the Old and New Testaments are a God-inspired witness; they witness to God's love for man.

The New Testament was written in the first century on sheets of papyrus (similar to paper but made from plant stems). The earliest fragment of the Gospel of Saint Matthew is thought to date from AD 70. The oldest surviving Gospel of St. John dates from the second century. The famous fourth century Codex Sinaiticus contains the entire Old and New Testaments together with two other books which are not in the Bible today.

At this time there were a number of other writings circulating that were believed, by many, to be genuine Gospels. The most well known is the so-called Gospel of Thomas (*right*), a complete version of which was discovered at Nag Hammadi, Egypt, in 1945 and dated to around AD 340. Other fragments of this work have been dated as early as AD 40, which is only seven years after Christ's Resurrection.

The Bible was put together by the Church and this process took many centuries. The Church didn't include writings just because they were old. The reason we have a Bible today is because the Church decided which writings were to be included and which excluded.

The Bible belongs to the Church and only she can explain the mysteries hidden in Scripture. She also teaches us directly. These teachings inspired by the Holy Spirit are called Tradition. Scripture and Tradition can't be separated – they exist within each other. Scripture is part of our Orthodox Tradition because it was our Church that put the Bible together.

Our faith is Bible-centred and our worship is too. The Gospel Book is the most important book in any Orthodox church. It's kept on the Holy Table all the time and we stand when it's read.

The Gospel Book contains only the Gospels of the four Evangelists: Matthew, Mark, Luke and John. We also stand to listen to the reading from the Apostle Book before the Gospel. The Apostle Book contains the Acts of the Apostles and the various epistles of the apostles. This reading is most often from one of the epistles of the Apostle Paul to the Christians of his time.

We also read psalms from the Old Testament in every Orthodox service. These psalms are found in a book called the Psalter. The most famous composer of psalms is the Prophet David (the one who fought Goliath) which is why he called the Psalmist. His most well-known psalm is Psalm 50 which we read in our morning prayers.

FREQUENTLY ASKED QUESTIONS

Which Bible translation is the best?

Unfortunately there isn't an official Orthodox English translation of the Bible. The best translation is the King James Version (KJV) which dates from the seventeenth century. Because this is a Protestant translation there are a few errors in it.

English Bibles like the KJV use a different version of the Old Testament to us. The Orthodox Church uses the Septuagint version which is actually available in English translation, but is very expensive. The KJV Old Testament is OK, but it doesn't include some of the books, and the psalms are numbered differently.

How should we read the Bible?

We can find the Bible readings for every day of the Church year on our parish website. Most of these are from the New Testament – the Old Testament is not read in church as much. Even if you forget to read them every day, make an effort to read the Epistle and Gospel for Sunday before you go to church. It only takes five minutes.

Some non-Orthodox churches run study groups in which everyone gets a chance to explain what the Bible means. This is not Orthodox. We must understand the Bible as the Church understands it. Reading the Explanations of the Gospel by Blessed Theophylact is an excellent way of doing this. We should also read or listen to the sermons of our bishops. We can find these on our Church websites.

> *The Son, born first of the Father without mother, is now born of a mother without father and hath granted me rebirth. Therefore, portraying in images both her that gave birth and Him that was born, I venerate them.*
>
> *From the Menaion*

SAINTS AND ICONS

To be truly Orthodox we must live an Orthodox life keeping God's commandments. As our guides we have the examples of the saints – those people who kept the Orthodox faith and became gods by grace. We ask the saints to pray for us to God that we might be given strength to follow the same path that they followed. We also praise God by honouring His saints as it says in the Psalms: 'Praise God in His saints.'

Among all the saints, we honour the Virgin Mary most of all because she was chosen to become the Mother of God. When we pray 'Most Holy Theotokos save us' we are asking for her prayers to her Son and God. The word 'save' in this context means 'protect us by your prayers from temptations.'

The Church on earth is made up of clergy, monks, nuns and lay people. We're all Orthodox Christians but we have different responsibilities. In the same way, among the saints there are bishops, priests, monks, nuns and lay people. There are saints who died in peace and saints who were put to death for their faith. Saints that have died for the Christian faith are called martyrs.

A saint is a living icon of God and an icon is an expression of this holiness using paint and gold. When we venerate the icons of the saints we are worshipping God by honouring His saints who are icons of God.

Icons are not religious paintings. Icon painters don't paint from real life or use their imagination. Instead, they follow a set of rules so the icon depicts not an earthly body, but one filled with the Holy Spirit. This is why icons don't look life-like.

The figure painted on an icon is called the 'prototype', a word which means 'first image' or 'original form'. St. Basil the Great says that any honour given to an image is transferred to its prototype. When demonstrators burn the flags of countries they don't like, they're showing their hate for the country (the prototype), not for the cloth that the flags are made from.

When we venerate an icon we're not worshipping the wood and the paint, but we're honouring the person whose image is painted on the icon. Leontius of Neapolis makes this clear:

> We do not worship the figures and images of the saints as gods. If we worshipped the wood of the image as God, then we would have to worship all other wood as well, and we would not throw the image into the fire when the picture fades, as we often do.

An icon also has an unknowable existence; it's not just a holy picture. The image is joined to its prototype in a mystical way and shares in the holiness of the prototype.

The Icon Studio at the Monastery of Saints Cyprian and Justina, Greece

PENTECOST ICON

Pentecost is the feast that we celebrate fifty days after Pascha when the Holy Spirit came down on the apostles in the form of tongues of fire and the mystery of the Trinity was revealed.

The semicircle at the top of the icon represents the tongues of fire descending on the apostles. They sit in a semicircle indicating the unity of the Church, but each is painted in a different posture, signifying the different gifts of the Holy Spirit that St. Paul describes:

> To one is given by the Spirit the word of wisdom; to another the word of knowledge by the same Spirit; to another faith by the same Spirit; to another the gifts of healing by the same Spirit; to another the working of miracles; to another prophecy...for by one Spirit are we all baptized into one body, whether we be Jews or Gentiles, whether we be slaves or free; and have been all made to drink into one Spirit.

The apostles are painted in inverse perspective (the figures at the back are larger than those at the front) to show that the Church is not an ordinary organisation but the Body of Christ. The empty place between the Apostles Peter and Paul at the top of the semicircle is the place set aside for Christ - the Head of the Church.

The icon isn't a historical depiction of the events at Pentecost. St. Paul wasn't a Christian at this time, but He is shown on the icon. This is done to show that the Holy Spirit came down on the whole Church and not just on the apostles.

Some of the people thought that the apostles were drunk when they heard them speaking in foreign languages. These people are represented by the figure of the old man at the bottom of the icon who also represents the whole world which was without faith. His age signifies that the world had been made old by the sin of Adam. His crown signifies sin which ruled over the world and the cloth in his hand containing the twelve scrolls represents the teaching of the apostles.

36

RESURRECTION ICON

This icon shows Christ descending into Hades. Other icons of the Resurrection show the myrrh-bearing women arriving at the tomb of Christ.

Christ is standing on top of the doors of Hades and leading Adam up by the hand. He holds a Cross showing that now the Cross is a weapon of peace and a symbol of victory, rather than a weapon of execution and a curse.

St. Nicodemos of the Holy Mountain makes clear that whilst Christ's body lay in the tomb His soul descended into Hades. However, Christ's body and soul were not separated from His divinity. In other words, although body and soul were separate they were still both joined with the Son of God:

> *His holy soul was separated from His body during His three-day death and descended into Hades, while His body lay in the tomb. However, the substance of His divinity was not separated from both His soul and His body. Hence, present in the tomb through His body, Christ's divinity tore death apart, and present in Hades through His soul, it freed the souls in Hades.*

Hades is represented by a black space in the middle of the earth. The nails and chains painted in white represent the bars of Hades that were used to keep mankind in prison.

The large blue-coloured oval shape surrounding Christ's body is called a *mandorla*, and symbolizes His divinity. The lines coming out from it symbolize the light of His divinity shining on the darkness of Hades. Christ's clothes have a yellow colour showing that His body is resurrected and glorified.

This icon is from the back cover of a Gospel Book which is why there are icons of the four evangelists on each corner. The Crucifixion icon is on the front cover. Russian Gospel Books have the icons the other way round.

FREQUENTLY ASKED QUESTIONS

Why do we venerate Relics?

A piece of iron in a fire glows red with heat and looks like fire but still remains iron. In the same way, the souls and bodies of the saints are made holy by the Holy Spirit. The bodily remains of the saints are called relics, and by venerating them we receive the grace of the Holy Spirit because of our faith in God.

We read in the book of the Acts of the Apostles that people were healed of their diseases by the handkerchiefs of the apostles and even from the shadow of the Apostle Peter. In the Old Testament, the relics of the Prophet Elisseus brought a dead man back to life.

There are many examples of miracle-working relics in the Orthodox Church. We can receive healing if we try to live our lives according to the teachings of the Orthodox Church and ask for healing with a pure faith in God who is 'wondrous in His saints.'

How does the Church decide whether someone is a saint?

When a person is 'glorified' (the term we use for the Church service that proclaims someone a saint), the Church is formally recognizing the belief of the people that this person is a saint. However, the bishops need to investigate the life of this person to make sure that their life and teachings were Orthodox.

Sometimes saints are only revealed many years after their death. Saints Raphael, Nicolas and Irene of Lesvos were martyred by the Turks in 1463, but their bodies remained hidden in the earth and the story of their life and death was forgotten. In 1959, these saints began to appear in visions to residents of the village near to where their martyrdom took place and also to many lay people, priests and the bishop. In these visions, the saints described their martyrdom and the place where their bodies were buried. Following the information that the saints gave, excavations were carried out and their bodies were found. In this way, these saints became known to us.

Didn't the Old Testament forbid making images?

God did actually order the making of certain images in the Old Testament such as the carved Cherubim over the Ark of the Covenant. However, he forbade the making of 'graven images' – what we would call idols or statues. Don't forget that in the Old Testament people couldn't see God. Any statue they made would be from their imagination.

After the Incarnation it was possible to see God and even to touch Him. We paint icons of Christ because we believe that He became man. We have icons of the saints too, because the saints are living icons of God.

Why do we kiss icons?

Some non-Orthodox churches have an icon on a wall as a decoration but people don't kiss it. The iconoclast emperor Leo the Isaurian had the same idea. Churches could have icons but they had to be high up. Actually, we don't just kiss icons – we venerate them. This means that we make the Sign of the Cross and we kiss the icon with faith and love of God. We don't worship icons though – we worship God with icons because we believe that Christ became man. The love and honour we show the icons shows our love of God.

> *The choir of saints have found the Well-spring of life, and the Door of Paradise; I too, have found the way by means of repentance; I am the lamb that was lost. Call me back again, O Saviour and save me.*
>
> *From the Pentecostarion*

The three most great luminaries of the Three-Sun Divinity have illumined all of the world with doctrines divine and true; they are the sweetly-flowing rivers of wisdom who with godly knowledge have watered all creation in clear and mighty steams: The great and sacred Basil, and the Theologian, wise Gregory, together with the renowned John, the famed Chrysostom of golden speech. Let us all who love their divinely-wise words come together, honouring them with hymns; for ceaselessly they offer entreaty for us to the Trinity.

From the Menaion

THE MYSTERY OF THE EUCHARIST

The first celebration of this Mystery was on the Thursday before the Resurrection and is called the Mystical Supper. When Christ had washed the feet of His disciples, He took bread, blessed it, broke it and gave it to the disciples, saying 'Take, eat, this is My Body.' Then He took the cup of wine, and having offered praise to God, gave it to the disciples, saying 'Drink ye all from it; for this is My Blood of the New Testament, which is shed for many for the remission of sins.'

When we receive Holy Communion we receive the Body and Blood of Christ. The word communion means 'participation'. We are joined with our fellow Orthodox Christians as St. Paul says: 'we being many, are one bread, and one body: for we are all partakers of that one bread.'

Through taking Holy Communion we are cleansed of our sins and joined with Christ as He says: 'He that eateth My Flesh, and drinketh My Blood, abideth in Me and I in him.'

The word 'Eucharist' means 'thanksgiving'. This mystery is a sacrifice of praise and thanksgiving offered to God by His people for the sins of all, whether living or dead. Christ is at the same time both what is offered as the Holy Lamb, and the One Who as the Heavenly High Priest makes the offering.

The Mystery of the Eucharist is celebrated in the service called the Divine Liturgy. The word Liturgy means 'the work of the people' because we all celebrate this mystery. On most Sundays of the year we celebrate the Liturgy written by St. John Chrysostom. On Sundays during Great Lent we use the Liturgy of Saint Basil the Great.

The order of the Divine Liturgy was passed down orally and only later was it written down. Over time, new prayers and hymns were added. In Orthodoxy the Liturgy has always been celebrated, and it will always be celebrated until the end of time.

LITURGY ESSENTIALS

The Divine Liturgy is divided into three parts:

- The Service of Preparation
- The Liturgy of the Catechumens
- The Liturgy of the Faithful

The following things are essential:

Priest and Choir

A bishop or priest is needed to celebrate the Liturgy. Often a deacon serves together with the priest too. To simplify things, in this chapter we're assuming that only one priest is serving. However, as well as this priest, there must be at least one Orthodox Christian present to sing the responses.

Prosphoron and Wine

In ancient times, the faithful brought the bread and wine to the church for the Eucharist and for this reason the bread is called a *prosphoron* which is the Greek word for 'offering'. The prosphoron is leavened, (leaven is another word for yeast) and made from pure, white flour. A prosphoron has three distinctive features:

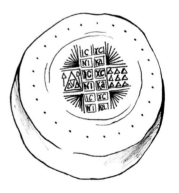

- It is made in two halves joined together to signify the two natures of Jesus Christ: God and man.

- It is marked with the sign of the Cross on top to show that this bread is for a holy use.

- In the four corners made by the arms of the Cross it has the letters IC, XC, NI, KA, which is an abbreviation for 'Jesus Christ Conquers' in Greek.

Antimension

The *antimension* (*see illustration on page 46*) is the special cloth on which the Divine Liturgy is celebrated. Relics of a martyr are sewn into it to remind us that the early Christians celebrated the Liturgy on the tombs of the martyrs. The antimension is also signed by the bishop.

THE SERVICE OF PREPARATION

The Service of Preparation takes place on a table called the *prothesis* which is a Greek word meaning 'preparation'. A cube is cut out of the centre of the prosphoron using a spear-shaped knife called a lance. This is called the Lamb and it is placed on a metal dish called a *diskos* (*right*). The Lamb will become the Body of Christ.

Wine and water are poured into the chalice. Smaller pieces are then cut out of the prosphoron to commemorate the Mother of God, the angels, the saints and all living and departed Orthodox Christians. These small particles are placed on the diskos surrounding the Lamb.

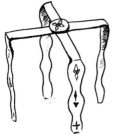

A metal asterisk (*left*) is placed on the diskos. Special cloths called chalice veils are then placed over the diskos and chalice, followed by a larger cloth called the *aer*. The priest then censes the gifts.

THE LITURGY OF THE CATECHUMENS

A Catechumen is a person who is learning about the Orthodox Church and preparing for baptism. The first part of the Liturgy is called the Liturgy of the Catechumens because Catechumens must leave the church at the end of it.

The priest, standing before the Holy Table, raises his hands in prayer to the Lord, and quietly reads the prayer:

O Heavenly King, Comforter, the Spirit of truth, Who art everywhere present and fillest all things, O Treasury of every good and Bestower of life: come and abide in us and cleanse us from every stain, and save our souls, O Good One.

The priest, making the sign of the Cross with the Gospel Book over the antimension, exclaims: '**Blessed is the Kingdom of the Father, and of the Son, and of the Holy Spirit, now and ever, and unto the ages of ages.**'

The choir answers 'Amen' and we then begin the great litany. The word litany is taken from the Greek verb 'to ask' because in all litanies the priest asks God for mercy on our behalf and on behalf of the whole world. For this reason, the choir responds 'Lord have mercy.' This litany is called 'great' because it is long! The shorter litanies are called little litanies.

After the great litany we sing Psalms 102 and 145. These two psalms paint a picture of God's gifts to us. At the end of Psalm 145 we sing a special hymn called the Hymn of Orthodoxy.

Only-Begotten Son and Word of God, Thou Who art immortal, and didst deign for our salvation to become incarnate of the holy Theotokos and ever-Virgin Mary, without change becoming man, and Who was crucified, O Christ God, trampling down death by death: Thou Who art one of the Holy Trinity, glorified together with the Father and the Holy Spirit, save us.

'Without change' means that in the Person of Jesus Christ, divinity was not changed into humanity nor was His humanity changed into divinity.

The choir now sings the beatitude verses from the Gospel of St. Matthew. 'Beatitude' comes from the Latin for 'blessed'; most of the verses begin with the word 'blessed'. We hear that we must be humble, repent of our sins, seek after righteousness, be kind to our neighbour, be patient and be prepared even to die for Christ. Hymns for the Resurrection or the saints are sung between the beatitude verses.

The Little Entrance

When the Beatitudes are being chanted, the Royal Doors are opened. The priest takes the Gospel Book from the Holy Table and leaves the altar through the north door.

The Little Entrance used to have a practical purpose. In the early days of the Church, when Christians were persecuted, the Gospel Book was not kept on the Holy Table but in a secure place for safety. When the time came for the reading of the Gospel, the clergy brought it into the sanctuary.

The Little Entrance represents the Saviour's preaching to the people. The candle which is carried in front of the Gospel Book represents John the Forerunner who went before Jesus Christ as 'a burning and shining light'.

The opening of the Royal Doors (for the Entrance) shows us that the Kingdom of Heaven is now opened to us. We now look upon the Gospel Book as if upon Jesus Christ Himself, setting out upon His preaching ministry as the choir sings:

> **O come let us worship and fall down before Christ. O Son of God, risen from the dead, save us who chant unto Thee, Alleluia.**

We now chant the Dismissal Hymns of the Resurrection if it's a Sunday and also for the saints of the day. On a Great Feast like Christmas we chant the hymns of the feast only.

The Trisagion

At the end of these hymns and after a short exclamation by the priest, the choir starts to sing the Trisagion: '**Holy God, Holy Mighty, Holy Immortal, have mercy on us.**'

At this time we should remember the words of the Prophet Esaias, who saw the Throne of God surrounded by the angels, who were chanting 'Holy, Holy, Holy, Lord of Sabaoth,'

Antimension

The Service of Preparation. The asterisk (*folded up*), spoon and lance are on the right of the chalice.

Inspired by this vision, the prophet cried out 'Woe is me! ... I am a man of unclean lips... and I live among a people of unclean lips.'

These words of the Prophet Esaias are important for us. We live in a world that has turned away from God. Part of the reason for this is that we ourselves are men of unclean lips. We are not living a genuine pure Orthodox Christian life. We are not leading people to the Church by our example.

The Epistle and Gospel

After the choir has finished chanting the Trisagion, the reader and choir chant a short verse based on the psalms called a *prokeimenon*. This is followed by a reading from the Epistles or Acts of the Apostles.

The priest censes during this reading. The censer represents Christ's humanity and the red-hot charcoal in the censer represents the fire of His divinity. The sweet smoke represents the Holy Spirit. The inside of the censer also represents the womb of the Virgin because she bore Christ, the Divine Coal, in her womb without being burnt.

The word 'Gospel' means 'good news'. Christ is this good news, He is the Gospel of our salvation. When we hear the Gospel we are in the presence of the Son of God. We see the priest, the icon of Christ, and we hear His words.

The Threefold Litany; the Litany for the Catechumens

In the Threefold Litany we pray for those with special needs, the sick and pregnant mothers. The choir answers each petition with 'Lord have mercy' three times.

In the Litany for the Catechumens, we pray that God will illumine the catechumens with the light of the Gospel and unite them to the Church by baptism.

During this litany we should pray silently for our non-Orthodox friends and relatives. We also pray for all the people of the world that God will have mercy on them.

At the end of the litany, the catechumens are commanded to leave the church:

As many as are catechumens, depart! Ye catechumens, depart! As many as are catechumens, depart! Let none of the catechumens remain!

The catechumens leave because they cannot receive the Communion of the Body and Blood of Christ. Their dismissal also symbolizes the Final Judgement when the sinners are sent away.

THE LITURGY OF THE FAITHFUL

The third part of the Liturgy is called the Liturgy of the Faithful, because only the Orthodox faithful can take part in the Mystery which is unfolding before us.

Many of the most important prayers of this part of the Liturgy are said by the priest silently. This isn't because we have secrets in the Church that are only known to the priests, but because these prayers are holy. In earlier times, these prayers were said out loud, but how different we are now to the people back then! Christians then willingly gave themselves up for martyrdom for Christ, but we can't even get out of bed to say our prayers!

The priest's prayers are a dialogue between God and the priest who is acting for us. The priest is talking with God 'one to one' as St. Germanos of Constantinople explains:

Then the priest goes with confidence to the throne of the grace of God and, with a true heart and in certainty of faith, speaks to God. He speaks no longer through a cloud as once did Moses in the tabernacle, but with uncovered face seeing the glory of the Lord...God spoke invisibly to Moses and Moses to God; so now the priest, bowing on account of the dreadful and awesome glory and brightness of the Godhead is initiated into the splendour of the life-giving Trinity.

The priest asks God to forgive his personal sins and the sins of the people. He also asks God for the greatest action performed on earth today - that the bread and wine offered to God may be changed by the Holy Spirit into the Body and Blood of Christ.

The Cherubic Hymn

After the litanies have finished, the choir starts to sing the Cherubic Hymn:

> *Let us who mystically portray the Cherubim, and chant the thrice-holy hymn unto the life-creating Trinity, lay aside all earthly care: That we may receive the King of all, escorted invisibly by the angelic orders. Alleluia, Alleluia, Alleluia.*

The Cherubim are angels who serve God and the words of the hymn remind us that we should be angels on earth.

As we listen to the Cherubic Hymn we should remember that we are members of the Church together with the Seraphim, Cherubim and all the other angels. At this time we should also join with them in praising God as Saint John Chrysostom says:

> *The angels above are glorifying; on earth the people in the churches are chanting a chorus offering the same doxology. The Seraphim above cry the Thrice Holy Hymn; on earth, crowds of people sing the same hymn. The heavens and the earth join together in festival. Heaven and earth join chorus together.*

During the Cherubic Hymn we 'lay aside all earthly care' and make a special effort to concentrate only on the mystery that is unfolding before us. We should ignore any distractions in church or distracting thoughts that might be bothering us. Listen to the words of St. John Chrysostom: 'As the Magi came out of Persia to go and worship Christ, so let us withdraw from the concerns of everyday life and make our way towards Jesus.'

The Great Entrance

The priest censes the church during the singing of the Cherubic Hymn. He moves to the Prothesis Table and censes the diskos and chalice which are on it. Then having put the aer on his shoulders he picks up the diskos and the chalice and leaves the altar through the north door.

As he does so, he commemorates the bishop and Orthodox Christians both living and fallen asleep. When he re-enters the altar, the priest places the diskos and chalice on the opened antimension, and covers them both with the aer; he then censes the gifts that have been offered.

The Great Entrance is an image of the burial of Christ; His Body was taken down from the Cross, wrapped in clean linen and spices and laid for burial in a tomb. The altar is an image of the tomb, the Holy Table is the stone on which the Body of Christ was placed.

The chalice veils represent the burial cloths and the aer the stone which closed the tomb. The priest and deacon represent Joseph and Nicodemus, who buried Christ and anointed His Body with sweet-smelling spices which are represented by the incense. The closing of the Royal Doors and the drawing of the curtain represents the sealing of the stone of the tomb and the soldiers that guarded it.

The Symbol of Faith

The priest now exclaims *'The doors! The doors! In wisdom let us attend.'* This exclamation dates back to the time when the doors of the church were locked at this point to safeguard the mystery from non-believers. This exclamation also reminds us to close the doors of our souls to every worldly thought and concentrate on what is taking place in the altar.

The curtain is opened as we read the Symbol of Faith to remind us we can only approach the Holy Mysteries through the true faith. It also signifies the opening of the tomb at Christ's resurrection.

During the reading of the Symbol of Faith the priest waves the aer over the Holy Gifts. This represents the over-shadowing power and grace of the Holy Spirit and also the earthquake at the time of Christ's Resurrection.

The Eucharistic Prayer *

As the choir sings **'Meet and right it is to worship Father, Son, and Holy Spirit, the Trinity one in essence and undivided'** the priest starts to read the Eucharistic Prayer.

The Prayer has three parts. In the first, we commemorate all God's gifts to man: the creation of the world and man's restoration through Jesus Christ. We also commemorate all His other acts of goodness, both those which are known and the unknown, visible and invisible. The first part of this secret Eucharistic prayer ends with the priest saying out loud: **Singing the triumphal hymn, shouting, crying and saying...'**

As the choir chants **'Holy, Holy, Holy, Lord God of Sabaoth ...'** the priest reads the second part of the Eucharistic Prayer. After offering praise to all the Persons of the Holy Trinity, he specially refers to the Son of God, recalling the Mystical Supper when Christ instituted the Mystery of the Eucharist:

...on the night He was betrayed, or rather gave Himself up for the life of the world, He took Bread in His holy and immaculate and blameless hands, and when He had given thanks, and blessed, and hallowed, and broken it, He gave it to His holy disciples and apostles, saying **Take, eat: This is My Body, which is broken for you, for the remission of sins.**

In like manner also, He took the cup when He had supped, saying: **Drink ye all from it: This is My Blood of the new testament, which is shed for you and for many, for the remission of sins.**

---

* In this section the prayers spoken quietly will be in italics and the words spoken out loud will be in bold.

Having in remembrance therefore, this saving commandment and all those things that have come to pass for us: the Cross, the grave, the Resurrection on the third day, the Ascension into the heavens, the sitting at the right hand, and the second and glorious coming: **Thine own of Thine own we offer unto Thee, because of all and for all.**

As this is being said, the priest raises the diskos and chalice and the choir sings: **'We hymn Thee, we bless Thee, we give thanks unto Thee, O Lord, and we entreat Thee, O our God.'** The priest now begins the third part of the Eucharistic Prayer:

Again, we offer unto thee this reasonable and unbloody service, and we ask, we entreat, and we supplicate: Send down Thy Holy Spirit upon us, and upon these gifts set forth and make this bread the precious Body of Thy Christ. Amen. And that which is in this cup the precious Blood of Thy Christ. Amen. Changing them by Thy Holy Spirit. Amen. Amen. Amen.

This is the most important and most sacred moment in the Liturgy. The bread and wine are changed into the true Body and Blood of Christ. This moment is called the consecration. The priest and everyone else in the church make a deep bow or a prostration to the ground.

After the consecration the priest commemorates the saints and especially the Mother of God. The next thing we hear is the exclamation: **'Especially our all-holy, immaculate, exceedingly blessed, glorious Lady Theotokos and Ever-Virgin Mary.'**

The choir answers by chanting the hymn of praise in honour of the Mother of God:

It is truly meet to call thee blest, the Theotokos, the ever blessed and all immaculate and Mother of our God. More honourable than the Cherubim and beyond

compare more glorious than the Seraphim, thee who without corruption gavest birth to God the Word, the very Theotokos thee do we magnify.

The Mother of God is praised immediately after the consecration because Christ became incarnate of her and she was the first to serve Christ.

Meanwhile, the priest continues praying for all those who have fallen asleep in the Faith, and for the members of the Church still struggling in this life; the bishops, priests, deacons and all Orthodox Christians living in purity. The priest then blesses the people with the words: *'And the mercies of our great God and Saviour Jesus Christ shall be with you all.'*

Supplicatory Litany; The Lord's Prayer; Communion of the Faithful

Our preparation to receive Holy Communion continues with the Supplicatory Litany that begins: *'Calling to remembrance all the saints, again and again in peace let us pray to the Lord.'* The last petition of this litany emphasizes that we are bound together by our Orthodox faith: *'Having asked for the unity of the Faith and the communion of the Holy Spirit, let us commend ourselves and one another and all our life unto Christ our God.'*

The sacrifice of Christ on the Cross has made us children of God which is why we can call on God as our Father. In the Lord's Prayer we pray that we be given the bread we need for our bodies and souls which is the Body and Blood of Christ. The priest then exclaims: *'The Holies are for the holy!'*

The curtain is now closed and the clergy take Holy Communion. Afterwards, the curtain and the Royal Doors are opened, and the chalice is brought out as the choir sings: *'Blessed is He that cometh in the name of the Lord. God is the Lord and hath appeared unto us.'*

At the Resurrection of Christ the stone was rolled away from the tomb and later He appeared to the myrrh-bearing women. In the same way, the curtain is pulled back and the Royal Doors are opened. The risen Christ, our Pascha, is then revealed to us.

After we have received Holy Communion, the chalice is placed on the Holy Table until the time when the priest blesses the faithful as he says *'Always, now and ever and unto the ages of ages.'*

The priest now moves to the Prothesis Table and the chalice is placed on it signifying the Ascension of Jesus Christ. The incense the priest offers represents the cloud which received Him. At this time the Holy Table represents the Throne of God the Father, and the Prothesis Table the 'place' where the Son of God sits at God the Father's right hand. The priest then exclaims: **Let us depart in peace!**

At the beginning of the Liturgy we prayed in peace and so we now leave in peace. The priest, standing in the middle of the church and facing the iconostasis now asks for the blessing of God upon us all: *'... for every good gift and every perfect gift cometh down from Thee the Father of lights.'* In other words, we are being sent out into the world having received the gift of the Holy Spirit like the apostles at Pentecost.

During the Divine Liturgy, we have travelled outside time through the time of Christ on earth. The Liturgy of the Catechumens represents the years when Jesus Christ was teaching, and the Liturgy of the Faithful the time from His Passion until His Ascension into Heaven.

FREQUENTLY ASKED QUESTIONS

Why can't women take Communion when having a period?

Old Testament law decreed that women were impure and ritually unclean when having a period. However, now we're under the law of grace and the reason women don't take Holy Communion at this time is spiritual.

Having a period is one of the consequences of Adam and Eve's fall into sin. Because of this, our souls are not as ready as they should be to receive the Holy Mysteries. Also, this time of the month can be painful and stressful making it difficult to prepare to receive Holy Communion by saying our prayers and fasting.

In some churches women stay in the narthex at this time and in others they enter the main part of the church but they don't kiss the icons or receive antidoron. In other churches, women will simply refrain from taking Holy Communion. We should just follow the practice of the church that we go to.

Why can't men take Holy Communion after an emission during sleep?

In the same way that women are not allowed to commune during their periods, men should not take Holy Communion if they have ejaculated during sleep. This is a rather annoying consequence of our fallen nature and it can be very frustrating and embarrassing, especially as it is unpredictable.

These emissions are common during adolescence and they may also be accompanied by disturbing dreams. As with thoughts that appear during the day, pay no attention to these dreams and don't worry about them.

Like periods, a nocturnal emission is a reminder of our fallen state. This is one reason why we don't receive Holy Communion on the morning after. Another reason is that we need to put out of our mind the sexual thoughts that we have dreamt about when having an emission.

I come before Thee, O Lord, with the cry of the Prodigal:
I have sinned in Thy sight O gracious Master: I have
wasted the riches of Thy gifts of grace. But receive me in
repentance O Saviour, and save me.

From the Triodion

THE MYSTERY OF REPENTANCE

When we were baptized and chrismated we became members of the Church and received the gift of the Holy Spirit. However, we have all become like the lazy servant in the Gospels who buried his gift in the ground and forgot about it.

How will we answer at the Final Judgement if we have forgotten the Gift of God we have received? We will be worse off than the unbelievers, because we knew the truth, but did nothing about it. We will have proved to be dead and useless members of the Body of Christ.

Being true members of the Church involves a continual struggle against sin. The word 'sin' means 'not making the grade'. The Apostle John the Theologian says: 'If we say we have not sinned, we make Him a liar, and His word is not in us. If we confess our sins, He is faithful and just to forgive us our sins and to cleanse us from all unrighteousness.'

We should live a life of repentance – a word which means 'a change of mind'. When we sin, we should struggle hard not to do it again and to change our life for the better. Christ Himself said that He came not to call the righteous but sinners to repentance.

The parable of the prodigal son is a famous example of repentance. The prodigal son, having run out of his father's money, decided to return to his father and repent for his wasteful life:

> I will arise and go to my father, and will say unto him, Father, I have sinned against heaven, and before thee, and am no more worthy to be called thy son: make me as one of thy hired servants. And he arose, and came to his father. But when he was yet a great way off, his father saw him, and had compassion, and ran, and fell on his neck, and kissed him.

We must confess our sins if we really want to repent of them. Christ said to the apostles after the Resurrection: 'Receive ye the Holy Spirit. Whose soever sins ye remit, they are remitted unto them; and whose soever sins ye retain, they are retained.'

Sins can only be forgiven in the Church because the Orthodox Church is the Church of the Apostles. True repentance and confession are called a second baptism because they wash our souls clean from the stain of sin.

We should repent but we mustn't despair. St. Paul says that godly sorrow is saving, but the sorrow of the world produces death. There is no need to despair on account of our sins because, as St. Cyril of Alexandria teaches, 'there is no sin which God cannot forgive for those who sincerely repent.'

Whatever sin we have committed, we should run to the healing power of confession. This healing power is one of the reasons that the Orthodox Church is called a spiritual hospital. Christ says that 'those who are well have no need of a physician, but those who are sick. I did not come to call the righteous, but sinners, to repentance.'

We are forgiven the sins that we say in confession. However, like medical operations on the body, sins leave scars on the soul as St. Cyril of Jerusalem says: 'The stains of sin also remain in the body; even if there has been a healing, the scar remains, so sin wounds both the soul and body, and the marks of its scars remain in all.'

This spiritual scarring explains why we feel guilty about the hurt we've caused others even years after we have confessed the sin. It also causes us to dream or think about our previous sins.

TEMPTATIONS AND PASSIONS

Most sins start as thoughts that we later turn into actions. Often we're troubled by thoughts that come into our minds from out of nowhere. These are temptations sent by the devil.

Christ tells us that the devil is a 'liar and the father of lies.' The devil and the demons are always trying to trick us into sin and these thoughts and situations are called temptations. This is why we pray 'lead us not into temptation, but deliver us from the evil one' in the Lord's Prayer.

Christ has defeated the devil, so he has no power over us if we take up the weapons of humility, prayer and the sign of the Cross. The devil and his demons don't know what we're thinking, they can only make guesses. Most importantly, God will not allow them to tempt us beyond our strength.

Thoughts that appear in our minds out of nowhere are temptations from the devil. They're not sinful. They only become sinful if we agree to them in our minds or enjoy thinking about them. It's a good idea to confess these thoughts if they have become sinful. St. Nicodemus of the Holy Mountain teaches us:

> You should confess too, the evil thoughts that you have, if not all, then at least those that bother you most, because just as the eggs of hens when they are warmed are given life and little chicks are formed, so also evil thoughts when they are not revealed to our spiritual father are given life and become acts.

If we're not careful we can develop what the Church calls a 'passion'. This is a sin that is rooted deep within us. Common passions are drunkenness, smoking, fornication, anger, pride and jealousy.

We should confess our sins and make a strong effort, with prayer and fasting, to stop the actions associated with the passions. For example, if we have a problem with drunkenness, we should try to give up alcohol completely or cut down our drinking drastically.

Eventually, we can start to control this passion that used to control us, but we will still be troubled by thoughts produced by this passion. By living a life within the Church, we will become more skilful at rejecting these thoughts and desires quickly.

If we fall back into the same sins, we must repent and start again. Some passions may stay with us to the grave, but we must keep struggling against them and trust in God's mercy.

HOW TO CONFESS

The priest is not a judge but is a witness to what we say. He listens to us confessing our sins out loud so that we can be joined again to the Church by the Holy Spirit that acts through him as a priest.

Priests aren't allowed to tell anyone what they've heard in confession. This means that we can speak honesty and freely and no one else will find out what we've said. It's important not to repeat to others what the priest has said to us in confession because the advice he gives us is personal and other people might need different advice. If there is something that is bothering us that concerns another person, we should discuss it with the priest outside confession.

Sexual sins are the most difficult to confess, but don't forget that priests have heard all kinds of things — they won't be shocked. It is important when we confess sexual sins and thoughts that we don't go into too much detail; we should just stick to the facts. We don't need to say exactly how many times we have done something or who with; we just need to give the priest some idea of whether it was an accident or something we have been doing for a long time.

We should also confess our sinful thoughts too. The Fathers say that confessing thoughts that we have had, but not yet acted on, helps protect us from falling into the sins of the flesh that these thoughts suggest.

Here are a few points to help us in confession:

- Turn over in your mind the things that you have done wrong since your last confession. Don't worry if you can't find the exact words to describe what the sin is.

- Don't blame other people in your confession or make excuses.
- Make a short list so that you can remember what to say when the time comes.
- Start off with the worst sins first as St. Nicodemos of the Holy Mountain advises: 'If you wish to defeat the devil who makes you feel shame, say first of all that sin which causes you the greatest shame.'

FREQUENTLY ASKED QUESTIONS

However hard I struggle I always commit the same sins. What can I do about it?

We tend to commit some sins more than others. Some are more inclined to anger than others, some are more jealous, some are more inclined to sins of a sexual nature. Going to confession regularly is vital even if we can't see any immediate benefit. If we put off going to confession we're going to add new sins to our 'usual' ones.

The spiritual life is like learning to ride a bike. Falling off is part of the learning process. Avoiding getting back on it will make things worse, not better. It's the same with confession. We keep going even if we always say the same things because confessing is changing us for the better. It's just that we can't see it yet.

St. John Chrysostom compares the fight against sin to chopping down a tree with an axe. The tree isn't cut down by a single blow, but blow after blow of the axe eventually weakens the trunk and the tree falls. Every time we confess we weaken the hold sin has over us. St. John also compares our spiritual state to that of an old crumbling rotten house: 'We remove the rotten parts from them and repair them. You have become old today because of sin. Renew yourself through repentance.'

I'm too embarrassed to confess what I've done.

Some teenagers stop going to confession because they feel unable to say some of the sins that they've committed. They've realised that they're no longer children and that going to confession as an adult is very different.

Hiding things in confession is a big mistake. Confession is like going to a doctor. Hiding our wounds will mean that they become infected and cause our spiritual death. Nearly everyone struggles with sins of a sexual nature so there's no need to feel shy or embarrassed.

Saint John Climacus compares these sins to a snake that has burrowed into our heart. The only way to rid ourselves of this snake is to confess any sin we've committed starting with any physical sin. These physical acts represent the tail of the snake. Confessing them is like pulling the snake out by the tail. We'll then be able to see exactly what kind of snake it is. In other words, we'll find it easier to fight off the thoughts and temptations represented by the head of the snake.

The fruit of the tree brought sorrow to the first-fashioned man, O Saviour, for Thou didst cast him out of Paradise. But when Thou wast nailed to the Tree* as a man, Thou didst lead him back to Paradise once more. Therefore I cry out to Thee O Deliverer: Set me free from all my sorrow, cleansing me by fasting, tears and repentance. O Jesus, the Saviour of our souls who art full of loving kindness.

From the Triodion

* *In hymns, the Cross on which Christ was crucified is often called a tree.*

THE MYSTERY OF MARRIAGE

Marriage is a great mystery as St. Paul tells us: 'For this cause shall a man leave his father and mother, and shall be joined unto his wife, and they two shall be one flesh.' St. Nikolai Velimirovich says that a pure and honourable marriage, in the fear of God, is a vessel of the Holy Spirit.

In Orthodox marriage the couple receive the grace of the Holy Spirit to support each other in keeping God's commandments and help each other into the Kingdom of Heaven. A marriage involves many different kinds of love. There is love expressed as friendship, kindness, affection and most importantly, the desire to grow together in the love of God.

The main purpose of marriage is spiritual, but there are practical reasons for it too. By being married we focus our sexual desires on only one person which helps us preserve our purity.

When a couple live according to the teachings of the Church and in a spirit of love and forgiveness, then the sexual union in which husband and wife become one flesh will be a true expression of the love they have for each other.

This doesn't mean that the act of sexual union can, by itself, lead couples to a higher state of love. As with all kinds of physical activity some people are better at it than others. For a number of reasons, a fulfilling physical sexual relationship may not be possible for every couple all the way through their married life.

Every married couple should be looking to raise Orthodox children so the Church can grow. However, not being physically able to have children isn't a curse like it was in the Old Testament. Many couples can't have children for medical reasons, but their marriage can still be fruitful and complete.

PREPARING FOR MARRIAGE

There are many different kinds of love. We should love God first of all. We should love our family. We should love our fellow Christians and even our enemies. However, even if we consider just the love between husband and wife we see that it is made up of different parts:

Sexual attraction: A marriage won't work if there isn't an element of sexual attraction between husband and wife, but any relationship based only on sex is bound to fail.

Mental attraction: We may be attracted to someone because of shared interests, or because we're similar people.

Genuine love: This love consists of putting the happiness of our partner before our own. It's demonstrated by kindness, consideration and lack of self-will.

Spiritual love: This is the shared love that the couple have for God and the Orthodox Church.

It's hard to decide whether we're ready to get married, but we shouldn't be looking for the kind of 'romance' we see in movies. Lots of successful marriages have very unromantic beginnings, but couples that fall head over heels in love tend to get divorced very quickly. However, if there's a doubt in our minds before we get married this is probably a sign that our choice of spouse is not right for us.

The Fathers of the Church advise people to get married at a young age to avoid falling into the sin of fornication. Virginity is a high calling and not everyone is capable of it.

Many non-Orthodox people delay getting married because they want to 'live their life'. In other words to live as they like without any responsibility – to live their life in sin. They still act like teenagers thinking that a 'party lifestyle' is acceptable for adults – it isn't. Being an adult is about accepting responsibility.

Others delay getting married because they can't afford it. After all, the average wedding in the UK costs £30,000!

There's no need for us to spend a fortune on expensive dresses, limousines and banquets for our Orthodox wedding. The Church service is the important part – everything else is optional.

We shouldn't rush into marriage though. We need to pray and take advice from our priest and our parents. We will never be really ready to get married because we can't prepare for it like an exam. The grace we receive in the marriage service will help us cope with the challenges that we will face in our married life.

Unfortunately, many couples these days don't seem to realise that marriage isn't just a romance and that it is sometimes hard to love, to obey and to forgive.

THE MARRIAGE SERVICE

An Orthodox wedding is not a private service to which we send out invitations. It is a Mystery of the Church in which Orthodox Christians join together in prayer as the couple are joined together in marriage by the Holy Spirit. In the prayers of the service we also hear about all the couples in the Old Testament and the blessings and joy that they received together because of their faith in God.

Orthodox and non-Orthodox weddings are very different. The most significant parts of the Orthodox marriage service are summarized below:

- The wedding rings are placed on the Holy Table before the service signifying that marriage has its beginning in Christ, and will end in Christ.

- The priest puts the bride's ring on the groom's finger and the groom's ring on the bride's. The couple then swap the rings themselves three times showing that they are entering into this marriage of their own free will.

- The crowns given to the couple are inspired by the olive crowns given to winners of athletic races in ancient times. They remind the couple of the spiritual race that they will run together, and are a symbol of the virginity that they have preserved.

- The cup of wine they share after the crowning signifies that they're bound together forever, and that they will share everything – their desires, joys and sorrows.
- The priest leads the couple around the lectern three times symbolizing that Christ will lead them into His Kingdom. The cross that the priest holds signifies the sacrifices that the couple need to make for each other.

FREQUENTLY ASKED QUESTIONS

Can I marry someone who isn't Orthodox?

The rules of the Church (called canons) say that we can only marry someone who is an Orthodox Christian. In the past, these canons haven't been followed strictly, but today the situation is very different.

Marriage is about sharing. Our shared Orthodox faith strengthens us and we share the same spiritual goal. We receive the grace of the Holy Spirit in the Mysteries of Confession and the Eucharist. Someone who isn't Orthodox cannot participate in these Mysteries, so there will always be a barrier between husband and wife. There are also practical problems too involving fasting and the raising of children.

We want to get married. Why can't we live together before?

Sexual intercourse is only a true expression of love when it happens between husband and wife. By living together in a sexual relationship before marriage we're disobeying God's commandments. We're living a life of sin rather than a life of repentance and separating ourselves from the life of the Church.

Couples who have sexual intercourse before marriage often separate after a few years because it was their sexual relationship that was keeping them together. After their marriage they give in to other temptations. They struggle to be patient, to be kind and to forgive.

In addition, by giving into sexual temptations before marriage we'll be more likely to commit the serious sin of adultery (cheating on our wife or husband).

Our marriage day should be the start of a new life. Our sexual relationship with our husband or wife should be new too. Our bond together will be strengthened by this newness. Our minds will be undefiled by previous sexual experiences, and we won't be comparing our spouse with previous sexual partners.

The Church understands that remaining a virgin until we're married is difficult, but it brings us great blessings both in this life and in the life to come.

Do I have to give up my career when I get married?

Most people reading this question will think that it's asked by a woman. Actually, both husband and wife should put their spiritual life before a career. We should work hard, but we shouldn't let ambition separate us from the life of the Church.

Ambition can also damage our family life. We shouldn't fit the needs of our children around our careers. Our spiritual responsibility to our children is more important than our career prospects.

Raising children in Orthodoxy is hard work and spiritually demanding. We need to bring up our children in Orthodoxy by being there for them – to teach them and set them an example of Orthodox life. However, lots of Orthodox women return to work when their children go to school; this isn't ideal but it's often necessary.

Must we start a family straightaway after getting married?

Being a parent involves sacrifice. We shouldn't delay starting a family just to advance our career prospects. Having said that, it's almost impossible for young, newly-married couples to afford a place of their own, let alone for one of them to stay at home and look after children.

It's certainly not ideal, but some couples delay having children until they have found somewhere to live and a steady job. The means that they choose to do this should be discussed with their spiritual father.

Isn't the idea of a wife obeying her husband old-fashioned?

Only if you think the idea that a husband should love his wife is old-fashioned too! We hear these words of St. Paul in the marriage service: 'Therefore as the Church is subject unto Christ, so let the wives be to their own husbands in every thing ... Husbands, love your wives, even as Christ also loved the Church, and gave himself for it.'

The husband must love his wife as much as his own body. He must imitate the greatest example of love – Christ's love for the Church.

Unlike in Protestant weddings, the bride doesn't vow to obey her husband in the Orthodox marriage service; she does it willingly because of her love for God. Naturally, a husband will never ask his wife to obey him when doing so would break the bond of love between them. Conversely, the wife would never want to disobey her husband because of her love for him. If arguments happen then the husband must remember to love and the wife to obey. If they both do this then arguments will quickly blow over and they can forgive each other.

FIVE SPIRITUAL WEAPONS

God helps us in many different ways to work out our salvation with fear and trembling. We receive grace by prayer, fasting, spiritual reading, obedience and giving money to the poor (almsgiving). We also use these spiritual weapons to fight temptation.

PRAYER

When we pray we stand before God; we talk with Him and we join ourselves to Him; we raise our minds to God and we give Him thanks; we praise Him and we ask Him for mercy. The Fathers say that prayer has three stages.

Prayer of the body is the movement of our lips as we say the words of the prayer. As we pray more regularly, we will be able to concentrate more and really understand and mean what we're saying. This is called prayer of the mind. Prayer of the heart is when prayer continues on its own and involves our whole being. This only happens when a soul is pure and free from all passions.

We can't start praying without ceasing unless we make a start! First of all, we should say the morning and evening prayers in our Prayer Book. We should learn some prayers by heart so that we can pray when we don't have a Prayer Book with us. Try to learn the 'Our Father', the Creed and Psalm 50.

If we're facing some kind of temptation or being troubled by thoughts we should make the sign of the Cross and say 'Lord, have mercy.' We should ask the Mother of God for her help by saying: 'Most Holy Theotokos, save us.'

We can pray absolutely anywhere as we can be attacked by the demons anywhere. The demons hate prayer, so we will face many temptations to stop us praying. We want prayer to become a good habit. Even if we feel no reward for our prayer we will be storing up treasure in Heaven by the very fact we're trying.

Prayer will always bring us benefits even if we can't see them. We need to keep asking if we don't receive what we request as Christ commands: 'Keep asking, and it shall be given you; keep seeking, and ye shall find; keep knocking, and it shall be opened unto you.'

There's nothing wrong with praying in our own words. We might want to pray for a particular relative or ask God for help in a temptation that we're having. Listen to this advice of St. Philaret of New York:

> In addition to reading the Church prayers, we must add our own prayers in our own words, praying for our own spiritual needs, for our neighbours and our enemies. Often, we cannot fully express our feelings and afflictions in the words of the written prayers. In this case, a living, sincere prayer in our own words is better, together with a confession of our daily sins and an expressed determination to struggle, with God's help, against those daily sins.

However, we should remember that God only answers requests that are good for our souls. Our way of solving a problem might not be God's way, so our prayer will not be answered in the way we want.

FASTING

Fasting is an essential part of the spiritual life of all Orthodox Christians. Our bodies and souls are linked together in a mysterious way and keeping the fasts of the Church helps us to prepare our souls for prayer and the worship of God.

Everything that God creates is good, but because of our fallen nature our bodies often work against our soul. Fasting is about trying to re-direct the body. It helps us transform our bodily desires for food and drink into a desire for spiritual things.

The Fathers say that eating and drinking too much excites the sexual passions. By fasting strictly according to the rules of the Church we're helping subdue our body to the spirit.

If we've failed to keep the fasts properly we should confess this. Young children, pregnant and breast-feeding mothers and the sick don't have to fast, although most will give up something. We should keep the following fasts:

Fasting before Holy Communion

We must fast from all food and drink from midnight before Holy Communion.

Lenten Periods

There are long fasts before the following feasts: Pascha, Christmas, the Apostles Peter and Paul and the Dormition of the Mother of God.

Fasting on Wednesdays and Fridays

Most Wednesdays and Fridays throughout the year are fast days. We fast on Wednesday to commemorate the betrayal of Christ by Judas, and on Friday we fast in honour of the Cross on which Christ was crucified.

OBEDIENCE

When, as adults, we look back on our childhood, the times when we were disobedient to our parents fill us with sadness, especially when they've departed this life and we can't apologise to them. On the other hand, the times when we obeyed instead of doing something we really wanted to do fill us with happiness.

St. Paul says to us: 'Children, obey your parents in the Lord: for this is right. Honour your father and mother; which is the first commandment with promise; that it may be well with you, and you may live long on the earth.' St. John Chrysostom says that those who do not honour their parents will never be able to treat other people with kindness.

We ought to hide our parents' faults and sins in front of other people and not cause them embarrassment. When we are tempted to criticise or make fun of our parents, we should remember the following story from the Old Testament.

Having planted a vineyard Noah drank some of the wine and became drunk. When his son Ham saw him lying drunk and naked in his tent, he called his two brothers to come and look. His brothers, however, behaved properly: 'Shem and Japheth took a garment, and laid it upon both their shoulders, and went backward, and covered the nakedness of their father; and their faces were backward, and they saw not their father's nakedness.'

Ham did not hide his father's nakedness, but mocked him instead and for this he was punished by God. Shem and Japeth, however, received blessings.

All of us have disobeyed our parents and used schemes to get around them. We promise that if they let us do something, we will do something in return. The devil used this argument when he said to Christ: 'All these things will I give Thee, if thou wilt fall down and worship me.'

We should honour and obey our parents out of duty, and not to get a reward. We should remember the words of Christ in the Gospel: 'When ye shall have done all those things which are commanded you, say, We are unprofitable servants: we have done that which was our duty to do.'

If our parents don't let us do something we should accept this decision. We shouldn't go and do it anyway. This is completely anti-Christian.

Lastly, we shouldn't cause divisions within our family by trying to get one parent to agree with us against the other. This is spiritually dangerous because we're conspiring to separate our parents whom God has joined together in marriage.

ALMSGIVING

The word 'alms' is based on the Greek word for mercy. Almsgiving is the act of giving money to the poor either directly or through charities. Christ praises almsgiving when He says: 'Blessed are the merciful for they shall obtain mercy.' We can give alms in a number of different ways and most

Orthodox parishes collect money to give to the poor. It's best to give alms to Orthodox charities as the money gets to where it's needed with the minimum of waste. Also, we know that these charities will not support or encourage abortion or any other practices that aren't Orthodox.

Many non-Orthodox people raise money for charities by doing special events and asking us to sponsor them. We can give them money of course (as long as the charity is not anti-Orthodox). However, doing sponsored events ourselves doesn't count as almsgiving. We're not giving money of our free will, we're doing something fun and asking other people to pay for it!

SPIRITUAL READING

Learning about our faith is a life-long process. Reading Orthodox books and the Scriptures is vital if we're to grow spiritually. It's not about learning facts though. When we read the lives of the Saints we're reading about people who have kept the faith; they became saints through living their lives in complete Orthodoxy – we should be inspired by these lives to do something more with our life.

We shouldn't read non-Orthodox spiritual books. The writings of 'saints' from other religions have nothing to offer us because their faith was not Orthodox. We are not saying that they won't be saved, we're just saying that their teachings are not saving. In many cases, these teachings contradict Orthodoxy so reading these books will harm us by leading us away from the true faith.

FREQUENTLY ASKED QUESTIONS

What is the Jesus Prayer?

The Jesus Prayer is 'Lord Jesus Christ, Son of God, have mercy on me, a sinner.' Everyone can pray the Jesus Prayer. Monks and nuns use a prayer-rope (*kombuscini*) when saying it which helps them to concentrate and keep track of how many prayers they've said without needing to count. It's good to have a prayer-rope, but we shouldn't just wear one: we need to use it!

What things can we ask God for in prayer?

Our prayers mainly involve asking God for one thing – mercy. We ask that He forgive us our sins. We also ask that God's will be done. When we pray before exams for example, we don't ask for a miracle; we pray that His will be done and that we are granted what we deserve and what is saving for us.

When we're ill we pray that God will heal our bodily sickness, but more importantly that He will have mercy on us at the Final Judgement. Sometimes illnesses can be good for our souls so if we don't see any physical benefit from our prayers we should understand that this illness is for our spiritual benefit. We should also remember to give thanks to God when our prayers have been answered.

Should we give money to beggars on the street?

St. John Chrysostom says that we show mercy on the poor so that we may receive great mercy from God. He also says that we shouldn't ask ourselves whether the poor person needs or deserves the money. We should just give it and we will receive a reward from God.

Society in the UK, however, is very different to the society that St. John Chrysostom was talking about. Today the government provides a safety-net ensuring that the poorest people in the UK are able to receive medical treatment. This wasn't available in the fourth century when St. John was alive!

The poorest people in the UK are usually homeless. However giving them money doesn't always help them. Many homeless people suffer from mental illness or drug addiction. If we give them money we're encouraging them to remain on the street rather than moving in to accommodation where they can receive treatment. Homeless charity workers are better able to help and support people with these problems.

Also, it's not a good idea to engage with homeless people when we're young. When we're adults we'll be able to see if a situation is dangerous or not.

If we really want to help the homeless, it's better to donate to homeless charities rather than giving money to people on the street.

I miss out on things that my friends are allowed. Why are Orthodox parents so strict?

Children have always feared missing out on stuff; it just didn't have a name back then. We should use the weapon of obedience to defeat this temptation. We shouldn't be ashamed to say: 'I can't come; my parents won't let me.' In fact, this obedience will bring a great blessing. Normally, the things we are 'missing out' on are physically or spiritually dangerous. They might even be illegal. It's natural for teenagers to want to try new things – this is how we learn to cope with life.

However, becoming independent does not mean being disobedient. It's something we have to go through like learning to walk. We need to work with our parents on this. They will let us make some life choices and help us get up when we fall down.

This temptation becomes less of a problem as we get older. We start to see that the things that we wanted to do as teenagers don't bring lasting happiness. Often they bring long-lasting suffering.

Blessed is the Christian who brings the fragrant freshness, and the strength of an undefiled body and soul into the bright wedded union through the Church, or who preserves to the grave the radiant purity of virginity and chastity.

Saint Philaret of New York

RELATIONSHIP ISSUES

These days, the word 'relationship' means a sexual relationship of some sort. As Orthodox Christians we should only be in a relationship with the person to whom we are married. St. Paul says that fornicators (those who have sex outside marriage or who commit unnatural sexual acts) have no place in the Kingdom of God:

> Do not be deceived: neither the sexually immoral, nor idolaters, nor adulterers, nor men who practice homosexuality, nor thieves, nor the greedy, nor drunkards, nor revilers, nor swindlers will inherit the Kingdom of God.

Many young Orthodox Christians give in to the temptation of having sex before they're married. This is a serious sin, but it's never too late to come back to the Church. St. Paul says that nothing can separate us from the love of God. The Orthodox Church holds open Her arms to receive us back again whatever we've done.

DATING

Dating is not traditionally Orthodox, but many pious Orthodox Christians manage to make it work. Having a steady boyfriend or girlfriend can be useful at university where casual sex is expected. It gives us a good excuse to reject the approaches of others.

However, we must think carefully before we begin dating someone. We've already said we can only marry an Orthodox Christian. If we're attracted to someone who isn't Orthodox, we have to lead this person to Orthodoxy by the example of our life.

We should explain how important our faith is to us and that we're not going to compromise. It's important to have this conversation early on and also explain that we're not going to be having sex before marriage. As our friend grows into Orthodoxy, we'll become closer and be able to support each other in preserving our virginity.

We shouldn't be dating someone if there's no way that we're ever going to marry them. Obviously we can't decide this straightaway, but if someone is firmly against Orthodoxy for whatever reason, then a marriage won't work out.

There are many dangers hidden along the road of dating and we shouldn't just imagine that things will be OK, or trust in our self-control. If we do, sooner or later, the demons will trick us and we won't be able to resist the urges of our body.

Everything we have said applies to boys as well as girls. However, girls are under extra pressure to have a boyfriend from a very young age. There's nothing wrong with calling a boy whom we get on with a 'boyfriend' if it's going to stop us being bullied.

However, we need to make sure that in trying to trick the bullies we don't end up being tricked by the demons instead. Some boys may be expecting some kind of sexual favour as part of their role as our boyfriend. We need to put them right straightaway. It's far better to be teased for turning someone down than to be pressurized into committing sin.

In every situation, being obedient to our parents is more important than our own wishes. This is especially true when boyfriends and girlfriends are concerned. If our parents forbid us from seeing someone we must obey them. However, things don't need to come to this if we talk to our parents and reassure them that we're aware of our responsibilities to God and to them.

VIRGINITY IN CHRIST

We should all struggle to be 'virgins in Christ' by living according to Christ's commandments and preserving our physical virginity. The Church regards virginity in Christ as even more blessed than marriage. St. John Chrysostom says:

> *Virginity is so great a thing that Christ, having come down from Heaven, was never so bold as to force it upon us; He demanded that we die for His sake, and do good to our enemies, but virginity He did not demand.*

In other words, Christ is not asking that we remain virgins forever, but He does command us to keep our virginity until we're married. This is difficult, but it will bring us a great blessing from God. It also has both spiritual and physical benefits.

If we're still virgins, we won't be troubled by thoughts and dreams about the sexual sins that we have committed. It's hard to understand when we're young just how disturbing these can be. They can go on for decades – the memories as fresh as though they were yesterday.

The physical benefits of preserving our virginity are obvious. We won't be at risk of catching sexually transmitted diseases, many of which lead to infertility in later life. Young women who take the contraceptive pill also have an increased risk of developing breast cancer. Women who are virgins will not fall into the trap of having an abortion.

We need to pray that God will enlighten and strengthen us to preserve our virginity. Blessed are they that marry having preserved their virginity in Christ. When we're tempted we should remember the blessings that we will receive for our struggle, and the sadness we will bring upon ourselves if we give in to this temptation.

STRUGGLING AGAINST SEXUAL THOUGHTS

We can't avoid sexual sins by mental struggle, avoiding intimate physical contact or making promises to ourselves; these things will help, but without the help of the Church they won't succeed.

We must live a Church-centred life. We must keep the fasts, give money to the poor, go to confession and take Holy Communion regularly. By doing this and trying to repent of our other sins, we're much more likely to be able to fight off these nasty sexual ones. If we realise that we're getting carried away with any physical contact we should use prayer as a weapon and call on Christ and the Mother of God to help.

Most of us are troubled by sexual thoughts that appear in our minds out of nowhere. They're at their worst during adolescence when our bodies are changing. These thoughts and images are temptations sent by the devil. The best thing to do is to say a quick prayer, make the sign of the Cross and forget about them! These thoughts only become sinful when we engage with them or enjoy pursuing them in our minds.

> *I have darkened my soul with lustful gazes and defiled myself with improper touching, and I have become vile in Thy sight. O Jesus, accept me as Thou didst the prodigal!*
>
> *From the Octoechos*

FREQUENTLY ASKED QUESTIONS

What things are we not allowed to do?

This subject is a difficult one for everyone and it can be embarrassing to discuss with other people, especially our parents. If we're not married, we should avoid all sexual activity including passionate kissing, cuddling and touching. Married couples should not engage in unnatural sexual acts, such as oral or anal intercourse. We should all avoid masturbation and watching pornography.

These last two sins are particularly difficult for young people to avoid as we're attacked on every side by sexual imagery. Pornography is extremely degrading to women and can alter our whole perception of the act of sexual union. The same is true with masturbation. We're turning what should be part of an act of love into a complete surrender to our sexual passions.

It's unusual today for people to move from childhood to adulthood without falling into one of these sins. However it's very important not to allow them to become a habit. If we do, we'll find it much more difficult to stop because they become rooted within us.

If we're having sinful sexual thoughts or have given in to these sins we must go to confession and try to correct our lives with the help of prayer and fasting. We mustn't ever give up or stop struggling, no matter how hard it seems.

Is having sex before marriage a very serious sin?

Yes it is, but exactly how serious depends on the person and the circumstances. It's a sin that people can fall into very easily if we're not aware of the danger. This is particularly true when we're young and if we've had too much to drink.

If we have fallen into sin, we should go to confession as soon as possible even if we don't feel ready. We may have lost our physical virginity, but by repentance we can regain our spiritual virginity. In other words, if we purify our souls of the stains of these sins, even though our bodies are no longer virginal, we can make our souls pure again.

Some priests may give us extra prayers to do or may tell us not to take Holy Communion for a certain length of time. The length of time depends on the circumstances. If our parents don't know about our sin, the priest may not stop us receiving Communion in case they find out. What he will expect us to do is to promise with our whole heart to stop any sexual relations and to act with as much care for our souls as we can.

> I do not have the fear of Thee dwelling in my heart and without conscience I have committed every sin of the flesh; and now I tremble at Thy judgement, O King of all. Accept me as I now repent.
>
> From the Octoechos

A virgin is not just someone who keeps his body undefiled by sexual intercourse, but someone who feels shame before himself even when he is alone.

Saint Isaac the Syrian

MODESTY

Dressing and behaving in a Christian way is called modesty. Our friends should notice that our faith is special without us saying anything. They might not know anything about Orthodoxy, but they should be able to see that we're different to the non-Orthodox. Christ calls us to witness to our Christian faith, so how look to the outside world mustn't be in conflict with this faith.

CLOTHING

Orthodox Christians dress modestly in church. Women cover their heads and wear skirts and men don't wear shorts or tight trousers. In some monasteries men must wear long-sleeved shirts and not T-shirts. Basically, we don't wear clothes which show too much.

We shouldn't dress in a way that is sexually provocative outside church either. Many modern bikini styles are too revealing and we wouldn't wear one at any time. We have to use our common sense though. We could get away with wearing a full coverage bikini on a family holiday, but at a Summer Camp we should wear something that is more practical and doesn't show as much. Basically, we should choose clothes that are appropriate for where we're going and who we're going with.

Being modest isn't just about clothing – we have to guard our thoughts and senses and avoid spiritually dangerous situations. For example, we wouldn't go on holiday to Pattaya and Magaluf which are famous for sexual immorality and drug abuse. These kind of places would be unsuitable for us whatever we were wearing.

Men are lucky because tight swim wear is out of fashion. Nevertheless, we should still dress modestly. Unless we're going swimming, we shouldn't take our shirts off in public. Many Orthodox men don't wear shorts either (unless they're playing sport). Men should grow a beard or a moustache too.

Finally, we should behave modestly even when we're alone. We shouldn't spend ages looking at ourselves in the mirror, or practice sexually provocative poses.

MAKEUP

There's nothing particularly wrong with wearing makeup from an Orthodox point of view as long as we're sensible about it. Some people with birthmarks or skin conditions use it to cover up. Others are happy to leave their skin in its natural state. It's really a matter of personal choice. We shouldn't wear lipstick to church at any time, and we should keep other makeup to a minimum.

If we're wearing makeup just for fashion, we need to consider what it's saying about us. Are we being modest or are we trying to fit in with the sinful world?

Wearing makeup makes us look older, but we still have to grow spiritually, mentally and emotionally. Being an adult is about taking responsibility for our actions. Our biggest responsibility is to keep God's commandments concerning modesty and purity.

TATTOOS

Until relatively recently tattoos were only popular among members of the armed forces and football fans. The tattoo showed the wearer's pride in their regiment, ship, or team.

Today, people get tattooed to satisfy some emotional need. They wear tattoos in memory of loved ones who have died, or to remind themselves of happier times in their life. Basically, they get a tattoo to feel better about themselves.

It's not surprising that self-harming is common among people with tattoos. Scientific studies have shown that people with tattoos are more likely to be sexually active at a young age; to have casual sexual intercourse, and to take drugs, than people without tattoos.

Tattoos are a permanent disfigurement of our body. Remember that our body is the Temple of the Holy Spirit. Having a tattoo shows the world that we belong to the modern 'look at me' culture that is deeply anti-Orthodox.

We should mention that Egyptian Coptic Christians are often tattooed with the sign of the Cross on the right wrist. The Copts have been doing this for centuries. It's particularly useful today as their churches are often targeted by Muslim extremist suicide bombers. The tattoo is used as a way of identifying Christians entering the church.

We don't have a tradition of Cross tattoos in Orthodoxy. We wear a Cross because Christ calls us to take up our Cross and follow Him. This act is voluntary and personal. We become Orthodox by baptism. We continue to be Orthodox by grace, by faith and by our works. This is why we choose to wear a cross rather than having one tattooed on us.

PIERCINGS

It's OK for Orthodox women have their ear lobes pierced. Men, however, shouldn't have piercings of any sort. Other kinds of ear and body piercing are not acceptable because they disfigure the body. In addition, these piercings also show support for a culture that it is not Orthodox. For example, many Hindu women believe that piercing the left nostril helps their fertility.

A nostril piercing isn't particularly dangerous, but top of the ear, septum and eyebrow piercing can cause infections, scarring and nerve damage. These extreme piercings are linked to a counter-culture which is anti-Christian. Scientific studies have also shown that people with extreme piercings are likely to self-harm. The danger and pain involved in being pierced is probably part of the attraction.

Mourn not for Me, O mother, beholding in the sepulchre the Son Whom thou hast conceived without seed in thy womb. For I shall rise and be glorified, and as God I shall exalt in everlasting glory those who magnify thee with faith and love.

A Hymn for Great Saturday composed by Saint Cassiane

ENTERTAINMENT

MUSIC

Music is a powerful medium because hearing is a very powerful sense. We must guard our hearing as carefully as we guard our senses of sight and touch.

From an Orthodox point of view, it's not easy to divide music into 'good' and 'bad'. For example, many classical operas are beautiful musically, but their stories are full of murder and adultery. However, these stories are so far removed from reality that there's no danger of anyone imitating them!

Popular music is more spiritually dangerous because it's the music of our time. It encourages us to follow the way of the world and to act sinfully. St. Basil the Great says that we shouldn't listen to music which encourages passions to grow within us.

By listening to pop music all the time we're slowly deafening our spiritual ears; we won't hear the voice of our conscience so clearly. In addition, it's more difficult to concentrate on our prayers and spiritual reading if we're listening to music the whole day long.

Popular music is linked to various anti-Christian subcultures. Rave music promotes illegal drug taking; heavy-metal music encourages a morbid obsession with death and suicide. Rap genres such as Drill glorify violence, drug-dealing and the brutal treatment of women.

Even mainstream pop singers target preteens with songs about sex acts and simulate them in their dance routines. Popular Christian music like Gospel isn't immoral, but the lyrics are usually heretical.

We could say that beautiful music is uplifting, while ugly music drags us down. Basically, if the music we listen to is interfering with our prayer life, encouraging our passions, or promoting some other faith we should stop listening to it.

BOOKS

Orthodox spiritual reading is a vital spiritual weapon for us. Reading good non-Orthodox books is important too. The more we read, the more we'll enjoy it. We need to choose our books carefully though.

We shouldn't read non-Orthodox religious or self-help books because the teaching in these books isn't Orthodox. Many books for teenagers are almost pornographic; reading them can inflame our sexual passions and put us in danger of suffering a spiritual fall. Most other books though, can't be categorised as either 'good' or 'bad'.

For example, some Orthodox Christians say that the Harry Potter books are dangerous because readers might copy the witchcraft in them. Others say that these stories are about good triumphing over evil and that the magic is the literary, fantasy, magic that we also find in the books of C.S. Lewis and J.R.R. Tolkien.

There are certainly worse books out there. Phillip Pullman doesn't hide what his books are about: 'I've been surprised by how little criticism I've got. Harry Potter's been taking all the flak…Meanwhile, I've been flying under the radar, saying things that are far more subversive than anything poor old Harry has said. My books are about killing God.' *

Reading one of Pullman's books isn't going to turn us into an atheist, but they aren't good for us spiritually. They also become a problem if we let them influence our way of thinking. The message of these books is that good and evil simply don't exist – life is meaningless. They're dark books that make people miserable; there's no joy or fun in them.

Obviously, we can't go through life only reading fun books. We will have to read things that we don't agree with. Reading good Orthodox books is much more important than avoiding

* www.smh.com.au/entertainment/books/the-shed-where-god-died-20031213-gdhz09.html

reading non-Orthodox books. The more we learn about Orthodoxy, the easier it will be to choose good books that we will enjoy reading.

TELEVISION

Having a television is inviting the world into our home. What most TV programme makers believe is entertaining, we believe is sinful. Watching immoral TV shows influences us in a bad way particularly when nearly every non-Orthodox person we know watches them too.

There are some good shows being made today, but we need to choose carefully what we watch. At best, television is a distraction. At worst, if can prepare the way for a serious temptation.

A lot of traditional Orthodox families don't have a TV for these reasons. Those that have one usually give up watching it during the fasts.

GAMING

We shouldn't play violent computer games or those that contain nudity or swearing. Even games without age restrictions can be harmful. The Apostle Paul says: 'All things are lawful unto me, but all things are not helpful: all things are lawful for me, but I will not be brought under the power of any.'

When a game leads us away from the life of the Church we have come under its power. If gaming has become a spiritual problem we need to deal with it before it becomes both a serious spiritual and mental problem.

Video and computer games are designed to be addictive. Too much game time can cause our relationships with our family and our schoolwork to suffer. Playing games instead of doing our homework might just be laziness, but it might also be the first warning sign of addiction. Reacting badly when our parents say that we're playing too much is another warning; addiction always starts with denial.

A gaming addiction can be devastating for young people. At the time when they should be making new friends and learning to cope with the outside world, addicts shut themselves in their rooms sometimes for days on end. They even shout at the screen as their 'game world' becomes real for them. They make connections with other players online, but can't connect with their own family.

A gaming addiction will cause us huge problems as adults, because if we don't learn to say 'no' as teenagers we will easily get addicted to things when we're adults.

> *Into the splendour of Thy saints how shall I enter? For I am unworthy, and if I dare to come into the bridal chamber, my clothing will accuse me since it is not a wedding garment; and I shall be cast out by the angels, bound hand and foot. Cleanse, O Lord, the filth from my soul and save me in Thy love for mankind.*
>
> *From the Triodion*

THE INTERNET

The invention of smart phones and social media have made the Internet a much more dangerous place. We learn about the physical dangers at school, but there are spiritual dangers too. We need to think very carefully about our Internet use. It's not only a waste of time, it has a corrupting effect on us and is a distraction from our spiritual life.

MOBILES

Using our mobile phone too much damages both our spiritual and family life. It distracts us during prayer and can make us forget to say our prayers altogether. It causes arguments at home when we use it too much.

It's easy to become addicted to our mobile if we always have it with us. Also, we're inviting the worst parts of the world into our lives. Bullying, for example, is more dangerous than ever before. Part of the reason is that victims feel as if the bullies follow them everywhere. If we carry our mobile phone everywhere the bullies *are* with us everywhere.

These days, mobiles are used as much for taking photos as for phoning and texting. However, we need to be careful what we're taking pictures of. This is particularly true if we're always taking pictures of ourselves. Taking selfies with our friends is fun, but we shouldn't become obsessed about it.

Sexting (sending sexual explicit selfies on social media) is completely wrong. Because we're Orthodox Christians we shouldn't pose immodestly for selfies either. There's no need for 'duck face' poses or taking selfies in our bedroom to show off our bodies.

At best, too much mobile use reduces our spiritual life to the minimum. At worst, we start worshipping the mobile instead of God; we care for it, we honour it and we turn to it for advice. If we are a slave to this idol we cannot be true servants of God.

SOCIAL MEDIA

Social media isn't actually 'social' at all! It doesn't help us make friends, it isolates us from people in the real world. We see this all around us. When people go out they sit around posting on social media instead of talking to their friends. This is the opposite of being social! Many young people find it difficult to talk to older people face to face because they're only used to interacting with people their own age on social media.

Social media tricks users into thinking that everyone else in the world is happy. It promotes a lifestyle that is completely beyond the reach of most people. It causes us to spend too much time on our mobile and demands instant replies and constant interaction. This means that we often post or 'like' in a rush without thinking properly.

If we post or like things on social media, we need to ask ourselves the question: Is this Orthodox? Christ says that by your words you shall be justified, and by your words you shall be condemned. This applies just as much to our social media posts as it does to what we say with our mouths. Listen to what Metropolitan Kallistos (Ware) says:

> *We live in a fallen world. We drag each other down. Each of us from the moment of his or her birth exists in an environment in which it is easy to do evil and hard to do good, in which it is easy to hurt others and hard to win their trust. If I know somebody very well, in ten minutes, if I set my mind to it, I could perhaps say to them things so cruel, so destructive, that they would never forget them for the rest of their life. But could I in ten minutes say things so beautiful, so creative, that they would never forget them? It is easier to speak words of bitterness, of hatred, than to speak in a memorable way words of love.*[*]

[*] L. Kisly (Ed.), *The Inner Journey* (Sandpoint: Morning Light Press 2006) p.155

Another big problem with social media is that most platforms are socially liberal and promote abortion and 'transgender rights'. Social media also promotes a mob mentality which bullies people into silence often by threats of violence. This mob is very powerful. University lecturers and UK government advisors have been sacked for writing things that people on social media didn't like!

In addition, a lot of stories on social media are fake news. They're either completely made up, or twisted to create the wrong impression. It's not just liberals that do it. Right-wing posters use fake news to target immigrants, for example.

It's a waste of time arguing about fake news because people who believe it won't listen to us. If we see something that confuses us then we should ask our parents, priest or Sunday School teacher. Between them, they will be able to find out whether it's true or not. The more we learn about Orthodoxy, the easier it is to spot fake news and the less it affects us.

PORNOGRAPHY

Having access to the Internet in our bedroom is physically and spiritually dangerous. The physical dangers are obvious. We must never arrange to meet someone that we only know from the Internet; adult child abusers often pose as children on the Internet in order to trap children into meeting them.

The biggest spiritual danger is pornography. These videos are really harmful because they're so hard to forget. We don't realise the damage they're doing at the time. St. Nicodemos of the Holy Mountain says the following:

> Those images which we have burned on to our imagination through our eyes we can only wipe out after a long time, much effort and sometimes not even then. Whether we are awake or asleep, they do not stop attacking us. In short, we grow old with them and we die with them. [*]

---

[*] Nicodemus of the Holy Mountain, *A Handbook of Spiritual Counsel* trans. P. Chamberas (New Jersey: Paulist Press, 1989) p. 89

Watching pornography is a sin made worse when accompanied by masturbation. We should struggle to avoid both these sins and confess them as soon as possible.

Watching pornography leads to serious mental and physical problems. There is medical evidence that teenagers who watch pornography become psychologically adjusted to the brutalizing and abuse of women. Their perception of women has been warped without them even realising it. Some even become physically incapable of having loving, respectful, sexual intercourse.

Watchers of pornography are not the main victims though. By watching pornography we're also supporting the abusive pornography industry in which performers are placed in danger of contracting sexually transmitted diseases or suffering serious physical injury. Every time we're tempted to watch pornography we should remember the suffering and deaths that it causes.

It's hard to resist this temptation even though we know that pornography is evil. There are practical things we can do. It's not a good idea to have a computer or a mobile phone in our bedroom. If we do, then make sure the Internet Service Provider's safe mode is switched on. Hopefully our parents will have set this up already.

Most importantly we need to pray to the Saviour to help us either with the Jesus prayer or with any other short prayer such as this verse from the psalms 'Have mercy on me O Lord for I am weak.' We should pray to the Mother of God and our Guardian Angel too. Having an icon next to our computer screen may help, but it's not a magic charm; we still have to pray.

If we have given in to temptation we shouldn't try to hide this snake in our heart. We must confess our sins as soon as possible. As we said earlier, these sins are very common, so we mustn't let our embarrassment stop us going to confession.

ADDICTIONS

Addictions usually start gradually, but they can spiral out of control especially when a person's harmful behaviour is encouraged by their friends. Our friends can influence us a lot when we're young. We must remember to obey our parents and never listen to our friends instead of them.

In the world, we're often surrounded by people who know nothing about Orthodoxy and care even less. Their speech is crude; they value everything we despise, and despise everything we value. We should separate ourselves from these people as much as we can. Listening to music or audiobooks on our headphones is a good way of insulating ourselves from corrupting conversations.

We've already discussed gaming addictions. In this chapter we'll discuss addictions that mainly affect adults: alcohol, drugs, gambling and smoking.

ALCOHOL

It's not sinful to drink alcohol. The first miracle that Christ performed was at the wedding in Cana when He turned water into wine. St. Paul says that drunkards will not inherit the Kingdom of God. We need to avoid drinking too much alcohol, either in one go or spread throughout the week.

Alcohol is a drug, and even a small amount can slow our physical reflexes. It also makes us aggressive and over-confident. Our perception of danger is reduced when we're drunk, which is why we tend to do stupid, dangerous things. Being drunk increases the risk of being robbed or even raped. When we first start drinking alcohol, we have to be very careful until we know our limits.

Alcohol slows our spiritual reflexes too; we may not see temptations coming until we have given in to them. How many times do we read stories about people doing stupid things under the influence of alcohol? Excessive drinking breaks up marriages and ruins the lives of the children of these families.

Obviously, it's unrealistic to expect that young Orthodox Christians are never going to drink too much. However, we mustn't ever get so drunk that we can't remember what we did the night before. This kind of drinking is sinful and leads to serious spiritual and physical dangers.

DRUGS

We mustn't let other people pressure us into experimenting with drugs. Don't be fooled into trying something to find out what it's like. Taking drugs is physically and spiritually dangerous; we don't need to find out for ourselves.

Illegal drugs are highly addictive and kill thousands of people every year. Drug abuse causes mental health problems including paranoia, psychosis and depression. Despite this, some people claim that cannabis is safer than alcohol. This isn't true at all. Moderate alcohol drinking is much safer than taking cannabis. Drinking a small glass of wine will not cause an adult any long-term effects. Smoking cannabis, just once, can cause serious long-term mental illness.

In addition, people that use drugs for fun are supporting criminal gangs that kill, torture and exploit people in drug-producing countries. There are also drug related murders of young people every week in the UK. Recreational drug users share the responsibility for the deaths of these people – they have blood on their hands.

If people around us are using drugs we're at a higher risk of trying them ourselves. Some recreational drug users also find it funny to spike drinks and food with drugs. We must make sure we don't leave our drinks or food unattended. Never take any sort of tablet given to us by 'friends' – no matter what they say it is.

The issue with drugs is just one of the reasons we choose our friends carefully. It's better to lose a few friends than become seriously ill. Even though drug taking is everywhere in colleges and universities, there will always be students who refuse to take drugs. We won't have any difficulty finding friends who think the same way as we do about drugs.

GAMBLING

Compulsive gamblers will risk losing everything to win back money they have lost. Even when they win, they're thinking about how they could win more.

Doctors argue that gambling is more addictive than drugs. Drug addicts have medical help available; many quit drugs each year because with the right help they realise how their addiction is destroying them. Gambling is more dangerous because it's attractive. People are looking to win something – they don't think about what they're losing.

The canons of the Church forbid Christians from taking part in 'games of chance' such as roulette, raffles and lotteries. This is why we don't raise funds by selling raffle tickets as some non-Orthodox churches do. In addition, we shouldn't bet on sporting events or card games. Basically, placing bets is not Orthodox. We must resist the temptation to gamble – even if it appears to be harmless.

SMOKING AND VAPING

Everyone knows that smoking causes cancer and is highly addictive. It's also a sin because smokers become slaves to tobacco and are failing in their struggle to control their bodily desires.

However, we shouldn't ever judge people that we see smoking or imagine that we're better than they are; smoking is highly addictive and some people can't give it up.

Vaping has become popular as a 'healthy' alternative to smoking tobacco. However, some liquids used in vaping release toxic chemicals that can cause serious illness. Doctors recommend vaping to people trying to quit smoking. Vaping is highly addictive so we shouldn't do it. There are plenty of other ways to stop smoking.

The Lord is good to them that wait on Him in a day of affliction, and He knoweth them that reverence Him.

Prophecy of Nahum

MENTAL ILLNESS

Lots of people claim to suffer from mental health issues today. Celebrities on social media are always talking about their problems with mental health. Most of this isn't real mental illness at all. It's just attention seeking by adults acting like children.

Younger adults today tend to be immature because they've been too sheltered as children and have always been given whatever they wanted. They're also very self-centred. It's all about 'me'; the needs and feelings of others don't really matter that much. As a result they haven't learned to cope with life's challenges and can't 'get their head around' things.

Real mental illness is very different and has a number of causes. It can be triggered by a chemical imbalance in the brain which can occur naturally or as a result of taking illegal drugs or even some prescription medicines.

People suffering from mental illness find it hard to control what passes through their mind. They might listen to strange voices in their heads; they might suffer from delusions (thinking something is true which isn't), or from some irrational fear or anxiety. They might be severely depressed or even suicidal.

We should ask for the prayers of the Church at this time. We need to remember the words of St. Paul: 'Rejoice evermore. Pray without ceasing. In every thing give thanks: for this is the will of God in Christ Jesus concerning you.'

Mental illness is difficult for doctors to diagnose because it usually starts gradually without many symptoms. Sometimes though it can start suddenly and require urgent medical help. These emergencies can be caused by childbirth, working too hard, or by some personal tragedy.

Unless it's a real emergency, we should receive treatment from the Church before going to our doctor. This is because we might be spiritually ill rather than mentally ill. Doctors can't cure the unhappiness caused by selfishness and disobedience.

Disobeying our parents makes us unhappy and is a type of spiritual sickness. Cutting off our own will and obeying our parents helps us grow spiritually and emotionally strong and able to cope with the temptations of life.

Problems like anxiety and depression might be caused by problems at school. We should tell our parents and our priest if we're struggling. They will help us practically and spiritually. It's not a good idea to take advice from friends or school counsellors because their advice will probably not be Orthodox.

Things are never as bad as they seem! We're all insecure as teenagers because our brains are changing and filled with strange and disturbing thoughts we've never had before. A lot of these issues are just part of growing up, and aren't mental illness at all.

It's important to pray too. For many centuries people have prayed to the Prophet Nahum and Saint Naum of Ochrid for help when suffering from mental illness.

SELF-HARM

Self-harming (usually by cutting) has become common among teenage girls in particular. Girls that self-harm are punishing themselves because they think that they're useless. This might be because they can't make friends or succeed at school. Self-harming can also be catching; if a popular girl in school self-harms, other girls tend to copy this behaviour.

Being a teenage girl can be a very lonely experience. Everyone else seems so happy. Why can't we be happy too? We need to understand that we will never be like everyone else because we're Orthodox. Even though we're sinners, we're special because Christ died for us. Our bodies are special too because they are Temples of the Holy Spirit.

Self-harm doesn't solve anything. By mutilating our body we're making things worse and not better. We must ask for the healing of the Church by confessing any thoughts we've had about self-harming. An urge to self-harm might be a teenage temptation, but it might be a sign of some more serious spiritual or mental problem. Whatever the cause, we should throw ourselves into being properly Orthodox.

EATING DISORDERS

Most girls try dieting at some stage even though most don't need to! Some become obsessive about this and starve themselves even though they're already thin. This is a form of mental illness because when these girls look in the mirror they 'see' someone fat. They're not seeing themselves as they really are.

Female fashion models have always been expected to look a certain way – super thin. The model Filippa Hamilton, for example, was told to lose ten pounds in weight despite being a size four at that time. At 5'10" and 120 pounds (1.78m and 54kg) she was technically anorexic. Hamilton was sacked because she refused to lose weight and risk her life. The company got around this problem by photoshopping her into the right shape. This kind of thing is a big problem. Girls feel pressurised into looking thin, but the images that they're trying to copy could well be fake!

It's a sin to be obsessed with how we look. Actually, our Orthodox Faith protects us from eating disorders; a diet only becomes an eating disorder when we disobey our parents. When we refuse to eat the food prepared for us, or lie and pretend that we have eaten it, we're being disobedient. We're not showing our parents the love and honour that God commands us to. Eating disorders can kill, but they don't have to reach this stage if we obey our parents.

FREQUENTLY ASKED QUESTIONS

One of my parents has a mental illness. Does that mean I will become ill too?

No. Not at all. There is some evidence linking our DNA to mental illness, but it can't be inherited like we inherit eye or hair colour. In fact, most scientists still think that the major cause of mental illness is our environment. This explains why even seriously mentally ill people can get better. It's a hard struggle, but it can be done.

Lots of us struggle with mental illness, but we have a huge advantage over the non-Orthodox because our spiritual life promotes good mental health. The Orthodox Church is a spiritual hospital for both the physically and mentally ill. In fact, people with a mental illness are often spiritually healthier than people who are sane (not mentally ill), but whose life is ruled by their passions.

Is demonic possession the same as mental illness?

No. Demonic possession is very rare and special exorcism prayers are read for the victim. These prayers aren't used for the mentally ill; the usual prayers for the sick are read. Even so, mental illness always has a spiritual dimension. This is why seriously mentally ill people (even nonbelievers) often say that they hear demons speaking to them.

How do we help people suffering from mental illness?

How we help depends on our relationship with the person who is ill. If they're a close family member we will have to be patient and help out as much as we can at home. Things will be difficult, so we need to be strong.

Trying to help friends, however, can cause dangers and temptations for us. If we're worried that a friend is about to harm themselves, we should tell a teacher. They will make sure that our friend gets the help they need.

THE NON-ORTHODOX

The true Christian Faith is only found in Orthodoxy. Truth and faith exist outside the Orthodox Church, but not together. This traditional Orthodox view of other Christian groups might seem harsh, but this harshness is in fact the most perfect love. The Church wants everyone to become Orthodox. This is the love of Christ, Who desires that all men be saved and come to the knowledge of the truth.

The Fathers say that salvation is only possible within the Orthodox Church, but this doesn't mean that all non-Orthodox people are going to hell. We would never say that, because God is the only Judge and only He knows the secrets of people's hearts.

We don't have space to discuss all the many non-Orthodox religions. We'll just talk about the two Christian religions that we're most likely to come across: Roman Catholicism and Protestantism.

ROMAN CATHOLICISM

The Orthodox and Roman Churches were united until 1054 but split apart because the Roman Church started to change the faith that had united the whole Church. We'll discuss some of these changes below.

The Filioque

The main reason for the split was that the Roman Church changed the Creed. The part in which we confess our faith in the Holy Spirit changed from: 'And in the Holy Spirit, the Lord, the Giver of Life Who proceedeth from the Father', to 'And in the Holy Spirit, the Lord, the Giver of Life Who proceedeth from the Father and the Son.' This addition is called the *Filioque* which is a Latin word meaning 'and the son'.

Adding three words might seem unimportant, but this new Creed contradicts Christ's words: 'When the Comforter is come, whom I will send unto you from the Father, even the

Spirit of truth, which proceedeth from the Father, He shall testify of Me.'

The Creed that we read every day in our prayers was approved by the whole Church at the First and Second Ecumenical Councils. The Fathers of these Councils stated that this Creed should never be altered, and the Orthodox Church has never altered it, apart from translating it into different languages.

In 808 St. Leo the Pope of Rome had the Orthodox Creed engraved on silver tablets and placed in St. Peter's Basilica in Rome. He added the inscription: 'I, Leo, put these here for the love and protection of the Orthodox faith.' Unfortunately St. Leo wasn't able to stop the spread of the Filioque in the west.

The Pope

At the same time as the Filioque was being added to the Creed, the popes of Rome were becoming ambitious and powerful political figures. They believed that the pope should be in charge of all bishops in the Christian Church.

One of the most famous popes of Rome, St. Gregory the Great, condemned the idea of having one bishop controlling all the others:

> I say it without the least hesitation, whoever calls himself the universal bishop, or wants this title, is by his pride, the precursor of Antichrist, because he is attempting to raise himself above the others.

Roman Catholics believe that the pope of Rome is the successor of the Apostle Peter. They often quote the following passage from the Bible to prove their point: 'I say also unto thee, that thou art Peter, and upon this rock I will build my church; and the gates of Hades shall not prevail against it.' They think that because Christ called St. Peter a rock, this means that the pope is more important than all other bishops.

However, they forget that shortly afterwards St. Peter denied Christ three times. The 'rock' Christ refers to is Peter's confession that he had just made: 'Thou art the Christ, the Son of the living God.' They also forget that several popes have been condemned as heretics by both the Orthodox and Roman Churches.

In Greek books, Roman Catholics are correctly referred to as 'papists' because of the devotion they have to the pope, and because he is the head of their Church. We should avoid using this word in England because our religious history makes it offensive.

For us, it doesn't matter how important the Roman Catholics consider the pope to be. The pope doesn't confess the Orthodox Faith so he can't be a successor of the ancient Orthodox popes of Rome.

Purgatory

Roman Catholics believe that our sins make God the Father angry and because of this He will punish us. According to them, Christ was sacrificed on the Cross to satisfy God the Father - to make Him less angry. However, they have a problem. We can't satisfy God completely by repentance, and we can't possibly have confessed all the sins that we have ever committed.

To get around this, the Roman Catholic Church invented a place called purgatory in which people are tortured in order to purify them of sins that they've not confessed. Imagine that during our life we were rude to our parents on 646 occasions, but only confessed it 435 times; after death, we would have to burn in the fire of purgatory for the other 211 occasions! The more sins that are left unconfessed, the more days we spend in purgatory.

Having invented this new system, the Roman Church then put it to good use. It's still possible for Roman Catholics to get days off purgatory by giving money to the Church, by repeating prayers a set number of times, or by visiting Rome.

The Immaculate Conception

The Immaculate Conception is the idea that the Mother of God was conceived without original sin. The Roman Catholic Church decided that because Christ is God, His mother had to be 'super-holy' too and different from all other women.

This idea is dangerous. Christ is God and man, and He is a man like us in every way except for sin. However, if His mother was a 'super-woman', and different to other women, then Christ would be a 'super-man'. Our human nature would not have been healed by the incarnation because Christ would not have become man like us.

Celibate Priests

In the Roman Catholic Church, priests have to remain celibate (they can't be married). This idea is not traditional and is a fairly new invention. St. Peter himself was married. In Orthodoxy, a married man can be ordained a priest, but single men are not ordained. A priest can't get married though; He must already be married before he is ordained.

PROTESTANTISM

Protestantism started in the sixteenth century as a protest against some of the worst parts of Roman Catholicism. Christians that call themselves 'evangelical' or 'born again' are technically Protestants but their beliefs are very different to those of the sixteenth century Protestants.

Saved by Faith

Evangelicals believe that they're saved by faith alone and that once saved they're always saved – whatever sins they commit. However, Christ Himself says that even those that work miracles and prophesy will not necessarily be saved. St. Paul did not believe that he was saved, but said that we should work out our salvation with fear and trembling.

St. James the Apostle says that 'faith without works is dead'. The works we have to do are spiritual works. We can't earn salvation by doing good deeds. We must have faith in God and struggle in our spiritual life by repentance, prayer and fasting.

Our salvation needs to be 'worked out' and 'worked on' by fighting against the passions with the help of the grace of the Holy Spirit. This cooperation between our works on earth and grace is called synergy. St. Paul actually says that we're co-workers (*synergoi*) with God.

The Bible and Tradition

Evangelicals reject any Christian history and teaching after a certain period of history, but the date depends on which evangelical you ask. However, they all agree that the Church started again when their particular group started. In other words they reject the whole Tradition of the Church. They don't realise that this means rejecting the Bible too because the Bible was put together by the Tradition of the Church!

Our Orthodox faith is Bible-based, but the Church is not limited by the Bible. Something can still be true even if it is not mentioned in the Bible. The word 'Trinity' is never mentioned in the Bible, but all traditional Protestants believe in the Trinity. St. Paul refers to the magicians mentioned in Exodus by the names 'Jannes' and 'Jambres' but these names are not mentioned anywhere in the Old Testament.

Millennialism and the Rapture

Most evangelicals believe in a thousand year reign of Christ on earth. During this millennium the Jewish Temple, animal sacrifices and Old Testament priesthood will be re-established. They also believe in a secret Second Coming of Christ to earth during which they will be taken up into heaven. This is what is known as the 'rapture'. Some evangelicals drive around with 'In case of Rapture this vehicle will be unmanned' bumper-stickers!

The rapture isn't just silly, it's not Christian. There will be no secret Second Coming of Christ. Christ says: 'For just as the lightning comes from the east and flashes even to the west, so will the coming of the Son of Man be.'

The idea of Christ reigning for a thousand years on earth (Millennialism) is based on a misunderstanding of a passage in the Book of Revelation. It isn't new. The founders of Protestantism condemned it in the sixteenth century.

We believe that the thousand years mentioned in the Book of Revelation signifies an infinite length of time. Christ's Kingdom is not limited by time because, as He says, His Kingdom is not of this world and will have no end.

Speaking in Tongues

The charismatic movement is big in modern Protestantism. The word 'charismatic' comes from a Greek word meaning 'gift of the Holy Spirit'. In their church services charismatics speak streams of nonsense words which they call 'speaking in tongues'. Some fall over and convulse, make animal noises or shout and laugh uncontrollably.

Speaking in tongues is mentioned in the Acts of the Apostles, but the apostles weren't speaking nonsense words. They received the gift of speaking in foreign languages so that everyone could understand their preaching. The 'signs' that occur in evangelical churches are evidence of demonic possession – they're not gifts of the Holy Spirit.

Health and Wealth Gospel

Some charismatics believe that being rich and healthy is a sign of being blessed by God. This is what one preacher says: 'The Bible says that He has left us an example that we should follow His steps. That's the reason why I drive a Rolls Royce. I'm following Jesus' steps.' *

These charismatics also believe we make things happen by saying that they will. They think that saying the words 'I'm healed' will actually heal them. In other words, God has to do

---

* F.K.C. Price, *Ever Increasing Faith,* Dec. 9, 1990 quoted in H. Hanegraff, *Christianity in Crisis* (Nashville: Thomas Nelson, 2009) p. 198

what we want. One preacher said: 'Never, ever, go to the Lord and say, "If it be thy will"… Don't allow such faith destroying words to be spoken from your mouth.' *

It's obvious that these teachings are anti-Christian. Christ says that it is hard for the rich to enter the kingdom of heaven. He also taught us to pray: 'Thy kingdom come, Thy will be done on earth, as it is in heaven.'

FREQUENTLY ASKED QUESTIONS

Why don't evangelicals honour the Mother of God?

Unlike the first Protestants, most evangelicals don't call the Virgin Mary 'blessed' as Christians should. In fact, we read in the Gospels that all generations will call her blessed. They think that honouring her is too Roman Catholic.

Modern evangelicals also say that the Mother of God was not ever-virgin because of this verse in the Bible: 'Then Joseph awoke from sleep and did as the angel of the Lord had bidden him and took unto him his wife and knew her not until she had brought forth her firstborn Son and called His name Jesus.'

In the Bible the verb 'to know' someone can mean having sexual intercourse with them. The word 'until' also has a different meaning to how we normally use it. When Christ said, 'I am with you even until the end of the world,' did He mean that He will leave us after the end of the world? Of course not!

Evangelicals also say that the brothers of Christ mentioned in the Bible are proof that the Mother of God was not ever-virgin. John Calvin, one of the founders of Protestantism, said that people who said this were ignorant. The brothers of Christ are Joseph the Betrothed's children from a previous marriage.

---

* B. Hinn, *Rise and be healed!* (Orlando: Celebration Publishers 1991) p. 47-48

May we pray with non-Orthodox Christians?

The canons of the Church are clear that we shouldn't worship with non-Orthodox Christians because we don't share the same faith. By worshipping with the non-Orthodox we are separating ourselves from the worship of the Church. We're also giving the impression that their faith is the same as ours. Sometimes we will need to attend non-Orthodox funerals and perhaps weddings. This is fine. We shouldn't attend non-Orthodox baptisms though because they involve affirming a faith which isn't Orthodox.

Can we join a university Christian Union?

No. Christian Union meetings involve praying with the non-Orthodox, and some require members to sign a Protestant declaration of faith. Obviously, we can't take part in anything that compromises our Orthodox faith.

How can we explain Orthodoxy to the non-Orthodox?

Saint John Chrysostom says that we should use everything within our power to convert the non-Orthodox, by showing them brotherly love, by offering them shelter, by being gentle with them and by all other means.

We should try to live according to the Orthodox Faith, by keeping the fasts, saying our prayers, going to church and struggling against temptation. People will notice that we're different from everyone else, but in a good way.

Even small things help. People will notice that we drink black coffee on Wednesday and Friday, but have milk on other days. Eventually they will ask why, and we can explain that it's because we're Orthodox Christians.

SCIENCE

Science tries to explain what stuff is made of, what it does, how it came into being and why it still exists. There are still many things that science is unable to explain, but these gaps in scientific knowledge can't prove that God exists because gaps can close even as others open. In this chapter, we're not attempting to prove the existence of God using science. Instead, we will try and show why science can't disprove God.

THE BEGINNING OF THE UNIVERSE

The Power of Chance

Some popular scientists say that the universe started by chance. Chance, however, isn't creative. People used to say that monkeys could type the complete works of Shakespeare if given enough time. We're not talking about copying, but inventing all Shakespeare's plays by typing randomly.

A computer simulation was run to test this idea, but even an enormous group of virtual monkeys could only manage 24 letters in the correct order and this took them 10^{40} monkey years! Even if we filled the whole universe with monkeys, we would run out both of space and time before they managed to write one play let alone the complete works of Shakespeare! There is also the problem of how the monkeys know when they've typed a correct series of letters. We will talk about this problem more later.

Chance cannot explain why the universe exists and why there is 'something' rather than 'nothing'. The physicist Paul Davies explains:

> *Suppose horses had always existed. The existence of each horse would be causally explained by the existence of its parents. But we have not explained yet why there are horses at all - why there are horses rather than no horses, or rather than unicorns, for example. Although we may be able to find a [past] cause for every*

 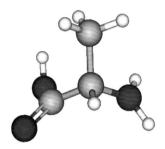

Above: The two mirror image forms of the amino acid alanine. *Right:* The two forms have a different arrangement of atoms in space; they don't match up when one is put on top of another. *Below:* The outer protein coat of the human papillomavirus (HPV 16). The green lines show the axes of symmetry.

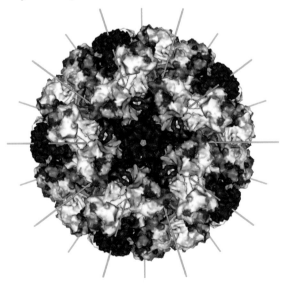

event..., still we would be left with the mystery of why the universe has the nature it does, or why there is a universe at all. *

Some atheists imagine that if we left 'nothing' long enough, eventually 'something' would be created. There is no scientific evidence for this idea at all.

Goldilocks Chemistry

The Miller-Urey experiment is often quoted as proof that life could have started by chance. In this experiment amino acids (the building blocks of proteins) were formed from simple molecules. Modern research has shown that the earth's early atmosphere would have stopped the amino acids being formed. The Miller-Urey experiment can't therefore explain how these chemical building blocks were first made.

There is another reason why the Miller-Urey experiment is not a reliable proof of how life might have started. Amino acids exist in two mirror-image forms called 'L' and 'D'. They have the same chemical formula, but because they're mirror images, they can't be placed on top of each other (see opposite). You can prove this by placing one hand on top of the other and getting the fingers and thumb to match up. It can't be done because hands are mirror images too.

Only 'L' amino acids occur in nature's proteins. However, in this experiment, every amino acid made occurred as a 50:50 mixture of the two forms: 'L' and 'D'.

The mirror image problem explains why it takes years for us to make a molecule that small organisms can make easily. Chemists are trying to put together a 3-D jigsaw, but having to make the pieces at the same time! The Bryostatin family of compounds produced by barnacles are a good example of the problem. The structure of Bryostatin 1 (*overleaf*) shows us how complex God's creation is. To make this compound,

---

* P.C.W. Davies, *God and the New Physics* (New York: Simon and Schuster, Inc., 1983) p.42

chemists must join the atoms together correctly and also arrange them correctly around each other in 3-D. The dark wedge-shapes represent bonds that are coming out of the page towards us, and the broken wedge-shapes are bonds that go into the page away from us.

Likewise, amino acids must be joined in the correct order to make proteins, but the protein chains have to fold around each other in a certain way too. It's mathematically impossible for this to have occurred by chance. The physicist Sir Fred Hoyle compared it to a tornado whistling through a junkyard and producing a Boeing 747.

Modern experiments that create molecules by 'chance' are cleverly designed to produce the right molecules. This is a kind of Goldilocks chemistry – everything is 'just right'. The temperature and pressure have to be just right, and the chemical intermediates must flow together at a time that is just right. The amount of time and effort needed to design these experiments actually disproves the chance theory.

Infinite Regression

The experiments that we've talked about make small molecules from the elements carbon, nitrogen and oxygen. The bigger question is: Where did these elements come from? Suppose they were formed by chance, where did the energy needed to make them come from?

This process of going back in time to find the ultimate beginning is called infinite regression – a term which basically means 'going backwards for ever and ever'. Consider this example of a child asking how a house is made:

Q: 'What are walls made from?'
A: 'They're made from bricks and mortar.'
Q: 'What is mortar made from?'
A: 'It's made from cement, sand and water.'
Q: 'Where does sand come from?'
A: 'It's dug out of the earth.'
Q: 'Where did the earth come from?' etc.

People who don't believe in God say that the energy at the start of the universe just happened to be there. They can't solve the problem of infinite regression.

Fine Tuning and Order

The idea that the universe came into being by chance can't be explained by the laws of physics. Many of the equations that describe these laws contain special numbers called constants. These constants must always have the exact same value or the universe would cease to exist. This idea is known as fine tuning. The Cosmological Constant, for example, is fine tuned to 120 decimal places; if it was slightly smaller or bigger the universe would not exist. The British physicist Sir Roger Penrose explains:

> Things get more and more random in the future... If you go into the past they get less and less random. So that means at the beginning of time, in other words at the Big Bang, things were highly organised. There's got to be fine tuning. There is incredible precision in the organisation of the initial universe.*

Scientists are always discovering organisation and symmetry in the universe. Frank Wilczek used his belief in nature's beauty

---

* www.youtube.com/watch?v=GvV2Xzh11r8

and symmetry to work out the mathematical equations that won him the Nobel Prize for physics in 2004. Although the maths might be new, the idea isn't. St. Athanasius the Great wrote this in the fourth century:

> *Since there is not disorder but order in the universe, and not chaos but symmetry, and not confusion but system and a harmonious ordering of the world, we must consider and form an idea of the master who unites and binds the elements together, bringing them into harmony.*[*]

There's lots of evidence of order in nature. The stomata on a plant leaf coordinate their openings even though they have no means of communicating with each other. The ion channels in cell membranes open randomly, but millions of random openings are coordinated to allow just the right amount of ions to flow one way or the other.

Order in the form of symmetry is also common in nature. The structure of ice is ordered and snowflakes are symmetrical. Some viruses are highly symmetrical too. The outer protein layer of the human papillomavirus (HPV 16) is made from more than 11000 atoms joined together to form 360 chains folded into 72 smaller units (*see picture on page 112*).

Entropy

Entropy is a measure of disorder. The more disordered something is, the higher its entropy. For example, ice has a lower entropy than water because ice is a solid and more ordered. Steam is higher in entropy than water because the molecules are higher in energy and move faster. Entropy is not just a theory – we can calculate the entropy of things.

Everything naturally moves from order to disorder. An ice sculpture increases in disorder as it melts and becomes water again. However, the reverse process doesn't happen spontaneously. No matter how long we leave it, or how much

---

[*] Saint Athanasius the Great *Contra Gentes and De Incarnatione* trans. R.W. Thomson (Oxford: OUP. 1971) p.103

we freeze it, water will not spontaneously form a perfect ice sculpture of Nelson's Column or the Statue of Liberty. We need to add order; we need to carve the ice!

The entropy of isolated systems, including the universe, is always increasing. However, the Big Bang theory we're taught at school assumes that things were in a maximum entropy state at the beginning of the universe. If entropy was at a maximum at the beginning, how has it been increasing ever since?

Sir Roger Penrose's solution to this problem is that the universe was created in a very special low entropy state. He has calculated the probability of this occurring by chance as $10^{10^{123}}$ to 1. To put this number in perspective, the probability of throwing thirty heads in a row is about ten billion (10^{10}) to 1. But the Penrose number is much bigger. It's not 10^{10}, it's 10 to the power 10^{123}. Sir Roger explains just how big it is:

> *This now tells how precise the Creator's aim must have been... Even if we were to write a 0 on each separate proton and on each separate neutron in the entire universe – and we could throw in all the other particles for good measure – we would fall far short of writing down the figure needed.*[*]

The Beginning of Time

The universe is always expanding. It's bigger now than it was last year, and the year before that. The universe was therefore at its smallest at the beginning of time. This means that there must be a point somewhere where the universe began and time started.

Physicists talk about the history of time, because there was a time when time didn't exist! This is interesting because the idea that time has a beginning is completely Orthodox. The phrase 'pre-eternal' that we hear in church services means that God has always existed, even before time began.

* R. Penrose, *The Emperor's New Mind* (Oxford: OUP, 1999) p.445-446

We believe that God created everything (including time) out of nothing. Physicists also tend to use the word 'god' as well, but they don't mean a God Who is worshipped; they're referring to the unknown force that pushed the universe from non-being into being.

DISPROVING GOD

It's impossible to design an experiment to prove God, so science can't say anything about God one way or another. For the same reasons, science can't explain why we find things beautiful, why we believe in good and evil, and why we fall in love. Scientists can't answer Prof. Sir Stephen Hawking's question: 'What is it that breathes fire into the equations and makes a universe for them to describe?'[*]

Most serious scientists aren't interested in disproving God – even those that study how the universe started. Most are just trying to do good science. Stephen Hawking, for example, didn't believe in God, but He wasn't anti-Christian. For many years he was a member of the Pontifical Academy of Sciences which advises the pope of Rome on scientific matters.

Popular scientists are nearly always anti-religion, but the 'god' they're trying to disprove is one that they've created themselves. They've built it using parts of religions that they don't like. They often use syllogisms like this:

The first premise: If science is true there is no God;

And the second: Science is true;

The conclusion: God does not exist.

Real scientists disagree with the first premise. The famous physicist Max Planck said that religion is closed to science because God has no cause (He just exists). The second premise isn't correct either. This is obvious if we think about it. Scientific theories change over time as new evidence is discovered. Even today's science is not always true. Scientists

---

* S. Hawking, *A Brief History of Time* (New York: Bantam Books, 1988) p.174

are under tremendous pressure to produce the 'right' results. Most don't cheat, but many ignore data or take shortcuts. In addition, researchers who contradict scientific 'group think' are given a hard time – even if their science is correct.

The Roman Catholic Church uses philosophy to prove that God exists and worries about whether God can make a triangle whose interior angles don't add up to 180°. The theology of the Orthodox Church is different.

We don't use human philosophy to explain what God can do. If we did, we would be saying that God is like us, but just better and stronger. Instead of philosophy we have 'communion' – God dwells in us and we in Him.

BIOTECHNOLOGY

Most physics and chemistry experiments are fine from an Orthodox point of view, but some biotechnology experiments aren't. Because the Orthodox Church teaches that human life begins at conception (fertilisation), we don't agree with experiments in which human embryos are destroyed.

Transgenic Organisms

The DNA in the nucleus contains the information cells need to make proteins. The section of DNA that codes for a particular protein is called a gene. Transgenic organisms are made by cutting out genes from one organism and inserting them into the DNA of another.

Using transgenic bacteria to make things like human insulin is fine from an Orthodox point of view. Transgenic crops that are resistant to drought and disease could help feed the poorest people in the world. This technology needs to be used carefully though because we don't know what damage transgenic crops will do to the environment. Scientists say that it's safe, but they don't know about long term effects because the technology is so new.

It's also possible to make transgenic animals. The first one was a sheep called Tracy. Scientists hoped that she would secrete a human protein in her milk which could be used to treat diseases like cystic fibrosis. However, when this protein was tested on humans it caused severe side-effects and medical trials had to be stopped. Somehow, the human protein that Tracy produced in her milk wasn't identical to ours.

Most Orthodox Christians are concerned about these experiments on animals. We can't support those that have no real medical benefit and which cause unnecessary suffering to animals.

Gene Editing and Silencing

Gene editing involves deleting harmful DNA. In gene silencing the harmful gene is not deleted but only switched off. Scientists use gene editing to remove the DNA that causes breathing problems in piglets. Patients with serious bacterial infections have been successfully treated using genetically edited viruses which kill bacteria. Gene silencing has also been used to stop apples turning brown when cut.

We would say that these techniques should be used responsibly – not just to make food look different or last longer. Scientists are also worried because gene edits of sperm or egg cells can be inherited. They don't know what damage this might do in the future.

Gene editing of humans is completely unacceptable to the Orthodox Church because embryos are destroyed during the experiments. Many atheists are against it too because they think that editing could be used to remove 'bad' genes from the population. This idea of not allowing 'inferior' people to have children is called eugenics and is completely un-Orthodox.

Cloning

A clone is a genetically identical copy of an organism. Bacteria and some plants can clone themselves. Growing plants from cuttings is also a type of cloning. Cloning animals, on the other hand, can only be done artificially. There are animal welfare issues with cloning, but the biggest worry for Orthodox Christians is that the techniques practised on animals might be used to clone humans.

Stem Cell Experiments

An embryonic stem cell can develop into any type of cell. Scientists often use human embryos for stem cell experiments which is completely unacceptable to the Orthodox Church. Not all stem cell experiments are bad. It's possible to do experiments with stem cells from human umbilical cord, and to change adult cells into stem cells. This latter technique could be used to treat badly burned patients by turning their healthy skin cells into stem cells and growing new skin from them.

FREQUENTLY ASKED QUESTIONS

Why do we object to human embryo research when it could stop people suffering?

Suffering is part of life. Medical experiments on embryos can't stop people dying, and they can't end suffering either. Supporters of embryo research claim that it will improve the 'quality of life' of patients, but what does this phrase actually mean? Just because a disabled person is unable to live our life, it doesn't mean they can't enjoy theirs. Their quality of life might actually be better than ours. We just have different ideas about what 'quality' means.

Should we avoid eating GM food?

There is nothing wrong with eating GM food from an Orthodox point of view. Some of us might be worried about the health aspects, but worrying too much about healthy eating can actually become a spiritual distraction. More importantly, organizations that campaign against GM food are often also anti-Orthodox. Greenpeace, for example, is a big supporter of abortion.

MEDICINE

Orthodoxy and medicine work together all the time. The Unmercenary Saints like Saint Panteleimon healed people using prayer and medicine without charging any money. In those days, there was no National Health Service or medical insurance! Most medical procedures and experiments are acceptable to the Orthodox Church. We will only discuss those that aren't.

IN VITRO FERTILISATION (IVF)

IVF involves removing eggs from a woman's ovaries and fertilising them with sperm in the laboratory. During IVF many embryos are either killed, or stored and destroyed later. This is completely unacceptable to the Orthodox Church, because destroying human embryos is destroying human life.

Some hospitals offer a modified form of IVF in which only two eggs are fertilised in the laboratory and both embryos are implanted into the mother. This procedure is generally acceptable as long as the sperm are donated by the husband and not by an anonymous donor.

ABORTION

Abortion is the deliberate killing of a baby in the womb. Abortions are carried out by giving the mother drugs to make her miscarry, or by physically crushing the baby and pulling it out of the mother.

Supporters of abortion try hard to hide the facts from women. They pressurise media companies into not allowing anti-abortion videos to be shown on TV. They're worried that if women saw what an abortion involves they wouldn't go through with it.

Abortionists call the child a 'foetus', but doctors trying to save a life call this child a 'baby'. This doesn't make sense. Changing a name doesn't change what something is.

A 24-week-old foetus doesn't become a 'baby' just because the mother wants the child to live.

Unfortunately, many women only realise they've killed a baby some years later. Anxiety disorders, depression, drug abuse and suicidal behaviour are all more common among women who have had an abortion.

Choosing to have an abortion is a serious sin. Sometimes, however, a baby might grow outside the womb, thereby putting the mother in immediate danger of death. In this case, doctors must act quickly to save the mother's life and the child will unfortunately die as a result. In this case, the mother hasn't committed a sin.

EUTHANASIA AND LIFE SUPPORT

The word euthanasia means 'good death'. The most common form of euthanasia is assisted suicide. Euthanasia is either murder or suicide and is a serious sin. Orthodox Christians who are seriously ill need our support, our prayers and our love as members together of the Body of Christ.

Although we reject euthanasia, we don't have to keep people alive artificially. Doctors may advise that the life support system that is breathing for a patient be switched off if they think that there is no hope of recovery.

Some of these patients, however, can hear and understand what is happening to them and go on to make a full recovery. We must ask our spiritual father before making any decision about removing life support.

Doctors may advise removing artificial feeding if they think that the person has no hope of recovery. This is a more difficult problem than simply turning off a machine that is breathing for us. Should people be allowed to starve to death? On the other hand, do we have to keep patients alive artificially when they would have died naturally if feeding had not been started?

ORGAN DONATION

Most transplants are carried out whilst the donor heart is still beating. To make this possible doctors have invented the term brain death – this is the idea that people can be 'dead' even though their heart is still beating. We would say that people who are 'brain dead' are still alive. In fact, sometimes they wake up – even as doctors are getting them ready for the operation to have their organs removed.

A heart for donation is always removed from the donor while it is still beating. There's another reason why we shouldn't have heart transplants. The heart is the centre of our existence and is mysteriously connected with the experiences of our soul.

We are taught at school that the heart is only a pump, but some heart transplant patients change personality and become like the donor. These changes in favourite foods, music and hobbies occur even though the patient knows nothing about the donor.

After receiving the heart of a seventeen year old black teenager, a white manual worker started listening to classical music. This is what his wife said about it:

> He's driving me nuts with the classical music. He doesn't know the name of one song and never, never listened to it before. Now, he sits for hours and listens to it. He even whistles classical music songs that he could never know. How does he know them? You'd think he'd like rap music or something because of his black heart. *

Of course, this man and his wife didn't know that the teenager had been killed on the way to a violin lesson – he loved classical music and died hugging his violin case.

Some people object to organ donation because the body is the Temple of the Holy Spirit and mustn't be destroyed. This is

---

* P. R Pearsall, G. R. Schwartz, L. G. S. Russek, Changes in heart transplant recipients that parallel the personalities of their donors *Integrative Medicine* Vol. 2, Nos. 2/3, Spring 2000 pp. 65-72

true, but the aim of organ donation isn't the destruction of the body – it's to help other people. It's not like cremation which deliberately burns the body like the pagans used to.

Most Orthodox Christians say that organ donation is OK as long as the heart has already stopped. However, it's important to keep our names off the donor register because at the moment it's not possible to opt out of 'heart beating' donation.

VACCINATION

The Orthodox Church is not against vaccination. Sadly, a medical error with the BCG vaccine in Romania in 2016 caused a fear of vaccination to spread. People also think that vaccines are made from aborted babies. Like most fake news, there's a tiny element of truth to this.

The Rubella (German Measles) vaccine was developed in the 1960s using lung cells from two babies that were aborted because their mother had caught this virus which causes serious birth defects and miscarriages. These cells were allowed to copy themselves, and the virus extracted and purified before being made into the vaccine. However (and this is very important), the vaccine doesn't contain cells from the two children, and they weren't killed to make the vaccine.

Non-Orthodox opponents of vaccination say that governments use vaccines to control people. Others say that vaccines disturb our 'energy flow'. This idea is found in witchcraft and various New Age practices such as crystal healing. It's completely un-Orthodox. It's no surprise that people who believe in weird 'alternative' religions also oppose vaccination. We mustn't allow ourselves to become infected with this virus of false belief.

Nearly all medical treatments involve some kind of personal risk. In the case of vaccination, we need to consider the risk to others as well. Spreading disease through a refusal to be vaccinated is spiritually very dangerous. How will we answer at the Final Judgement if our actions have caused others to become seriously ill, suffer and die?

FREQUENTLY ASKED QUESTIONS

Is abortion always wrong? Even in cases of rape?

The Orthodox Church doesn't approve of abortion even following rape. This might seem very cruel, but ending human life is not a solution for suffering. In fact, abortion causes more suffering. Doctors have known for years that abortion can cause long-term physical and psychological damage to the mother. Why add more traumas to a woman who has already suffered enough?

Of course, the victim doesn't have to raise the child. Some women choose to, others offer the child for adoption to bring joy to a childless couple.

Victims of rape are traumatized and may opt for an abortion while the balance of their mind is disturbed. The Church can never approve of this, but would never openly condemn the victim as happened in the Roman Catholic Church recently. Everything would be discussed secretly in confession.

Should we get the HPV vaccine?

People who have multiple sexual partners risk developing cervical and mouth cancer via a virus called HPV. Traditional Orthodox Christians are at a very low risk of catching HPV because we don't believe in having sex before marriage. Because of this, the HPV vaccine is optional for us. The science isn't completely clear yet, but it's a good idea to get vaccinated against HPV if we have a genetic history of these cancers in our family. Some Christians say that this vaccine makes teenagers more likely to have sex, but being vaccinated isn't going to change what we believe!

Can we give blood?

We should give blood if we are able. We can also donate bone marrow, a kidney or part of our liver. Donating part of our organs is a obviously very serious matter and we need to discuss it with our relatives, doctors and our spiritual father.

EVOLUTION

Charles Darwin's *The Origin of Species* was first published in 1859. Today at school we are taught an updated version of Darwin's theory of evolution called Neo-Darwinism. There are other evolutionary theories too, but in this chapter when we refer to evolution we mean Neo-Darwinism.

According to this theory life started by a series of random events in which cells were formed from atoms. Evolutionists can't explain how this occurred as one evolutionist admits: 'Pick up any biochemistry textbook, and you will find perhaps two or three references to evolution. Turn to one of these and you will be lucky to find anything better than "evolution selects the fittest molecules for their biological function."'* This inability to explain how things happened is evolution's biggest weakness.

DNA AND GENES

A gene is a small section of DNA that contains instructions the cell needs to make a particular protein. Evolutionists say that everything we 'are' – our beliefs, our likes and dislikes – is down to our genes. Richard Dawkins goes so far as to say that genes are both selfish and immortal, but there's no scientific evidence for this at all.

Genes aren't like atoms that can float about on their own and still function. Genes are only as powerful as the cell allows them to be. To be truly selfish, genes would need to be able to copy themselves. Genes are copied by protein-based biological copying machines. However, these proteins can't be made by accident. Each one is made following precise instructions found in our genes. In other words, DNA holds the recipe for making proteins, yet that information cannot be copied without proteins. Which came first? The chicken (the protein) or the egg (the DNA)?

* Andrew Pomiankowski, The God of the Tiny Gaps *New Scientist* No. 2047, 14/09/1996. Retrieved from www.newscientist.com

Genes can't be selfish because they can't act on their own. In fact, genes only work when they're acting together inside a cell. They can't live outside a cell so they can't be immortal either!

Over the last ten years, scientists have learned that genes are not as powerful as they once thought. Only some of our DNA is in the form of genes. The DNA in between the genes is called Junk DNA because it doesn't seem to do anything. According to evolutionists, Junk DNA is evidence of failed attempts to evolve new genes.

Recently, however, scientists involved in the ENCODE project at Stanford University have discovered that Junk DNA isn't junk at all, but contains instructions that turn certain genes on or off. Scientists are now investigating how this Junk DNA could be used in treating various diseases.

MUTATIONS AND NATURAL SELECTION

Genes are copied in our bodies all the time and errors in this process are called mutations. Evolutionary theory says that mutations produce new genes and eventually, if enough mutations occur, a new species will be formed.

These 'good' genes are chosen by natural selection. Darwin's idea of natural selection is also called 'survival of the fittest'. It's a fairly obvious theory. If a herd of zebras is attacked by lions, a three-legged zebra is more likely to be killed and eaten because it's slower than the four-legged zebras.

Natural selection is true because we can observe it scientifically, but it can't create things from nothing. Natural selection explains why weak organisms die, but it can't explain how 'good' genes are chosen because genes are invisible to the power of natural selection. It's a bit like trying to see the inside of a plant cell by looking at a carrot through a magnifying glass.

Genes can only be 'seen' by natural selection if they cause some change in the organism. In general, though, mutations that cause big changes are dangerous and lead to sickness and death.

Even small useful mutations have a downside. Canadian Kermode Bears look like polar bears due to a small mutation. Their colour makes them better at catching fish than black bears because they're well camouflaged against the water (*see page 130*). However, they're more likely to be shot by hunters because they're badly camouflaged against dark rocks and trees.

A similar kind of thing happens in bacteria. A mutation causes some bacteria to make penicillinase (the enzyme that destroys penicillin). However, when there's no penicillin around, these bacteria are weaker than their competitors because they wasting energy making penicillinase.

Mutations cause variation within a species, but they can't explain how one species changes into another. Scientists have studied every possible DNA mutation of the fruit fly and found that none would be useful for evolution. In other words, mutations could never transform the fruit fly into something else. The scientists won a Nobel Prize for this work in 1995.

RANDOMNESS

Not only do evolutionists believe that mutations can change one species into another, but they also believe that random mutations can explain how life evolved from atoms. Apparently, millions of random small mutations over millions of years can combine to produce a change that can be naturally selected.

However, there's a big problem here. Somehow the organism must 'know' that it is carrying a small mutation that in a million years might be useful. Evolution, though, is meant to be completely random. It doesn't know where it's going or what it is aiming to achieve. It has no plan.

Let's consider the room full of monkeys again. Everyone accepts that the monkeys could never type the complete

Two mice with identical DNA. Environmental factors have switched on a gene in the mouse on the left.

A Kermode Bear fishing. A DNA mutation causes this bear to have white rather than black fur.

works of Shakespeare randomly. To get around this Richard Dawkins has suggested that each monkey has a small target phrase and every time they type a letter, their work is checked for correctness against the target phrase.

However, for this to work, there must be a head monkey in the room reading the complete works of Shakespeare! He must be checking the typing and rejecting incorrect words. The monkeys are therefore working to a plan – even if each letter is typed randomly the overall process isn't random at all.

GIVE THINGS ENOUGH TIME...

Random evolution means waiting for the right mutations to come together by chance. However, one mutation isn't any good. The same mutation needs to happen again and again so that it can become fixed within a population.

This fixing takes a long time. Waiting for enough small mutations to occur randomly takes a long time. Too long in fact. According to evolutionary theory, humans and chimps share a common ancestor. Humans evolved from this ancestor over the course of six million years. A lot must have happened over this time because humans and chimps have around 35 million differences in their DNA. However, calculations by evolutionists have shown that it would take 216 million years for just one pair of mutations to become fixed.

NEW EVOLUTIONARY THEORIES

We're taught at school that acquired characteristics can't be passed on to our children. For example, blacksmiths are normally strong men with one arm much more muscled than the other. The blacksmith's children, though, will not be born with one arm bigger than the other.

In fact, new research has shown that genes can be turned on and off by our environment, meaning that some acquired characteristics can be inherited. For example, a female gerbil will give birth to more male gerbils than female if she was born from a litter of mainly male gerbils. She will also be more aggressive than the average female.

These changes occur because the baby male gerbils secrete the male hormone testosterone in their mother's womb. This causes changes in the egg cells of the baby female gerbils.

This phenomenon is called epigenetic inheritance and occurs because DNA can be chemically 'flagged' by things in the environment. These flags can be inherited, but they don't actually change our genes. If we call DNA the letters of the alphabet, epigenetic markers are punctuation marks; they add expression and colour to the DNA code.

The photo on page 130 shows an example of epigentic inheritance. The two mice have identical DNA, but were implanted as embryos into two female mice on different diets. Its mother's diet has switched on the *agouti* gene in the mouse on the left causing weight gain, diabetes and the yellow fur colour. The agouti gene in the normal looking mouse on the right is still switched off.

Epigenetics completely contradicts the traditional theory of evolution, but it could explain how organisms can adapt quickly to their environment. Epigenetic inheritance might speed up natural selection and help evolutionists solve the 'waiting time' problem. Epigenetics helps us too. It's clear that the theory of evolution we're taught at school is scientifically incorrect. No one can claim now that the theory has been completely proved and that it can disprove God.

FOSSIL EVIDENCE

Fossils cause evolutionists a lot of problems. We imagine that all fossils are found intact like the skeletons we see in museums. It's just not like that. Palaeontologists (scientists that study fossils) have to collect and sort out the fossils which are normally scattered about over a large area.

Brachiopod fossils, however, tend to be well-preserved. The evolutionist Stephen Jay Gould noted that species don't evolve from lower life forms – they're already fully formed. When they disappear from the fossil record, they look much the same as they did when they first appeared.

Although older fossils (the ones that are found deeper in the earth) are simpler than newer fossils, this progression from simpler to more complex isn't smooth. There are several events in geological time called explosions when new organisms suddenly appear from nowhere. The most well known is the Cambrian Explosion.

The Cambrian layer is a layer of the earth believed by geologists to be around 530 million years old. The Cambrian fossils are the complete opposite of what is predicted by evolutionary theory. Even the famous atheist and evolutionist Richard Dawkins realises that this is a problem:

> We find many of them [Cambrian fossils] already in an advanced state of evolution, the very first time they appear. It is as though they were just planted there, without any evolutionary history. Needless to say, this appearance of sudden planting has delighted creationists.[*]

Putting fossils in order is a difficult business. Finding a line of similar fossils doesn't mean that one species evolved from another. It might make sense if they did, but fossils can't prove it. Henry Gee, the editor of Nature magazine, explains:

> No fossil is buried with its birth certificate... To take a line of fossils and claim that they represent a lineage is not a scientific hypothesis that can be tested, but an assertion that carries that same validity as a bedtime story – amusing, perhaps instructive, but not scientific.[**]

JUST-SO STORIES

These family trees are based on just-so stories. Famous examples include dinosaurs changing into birds by leaping

[*] R. Dawkins, *The Blind Watchmaker* (London: W.W. Norton & Company, 1987), p. 229
[**] H. Gee, *In Search of Deep Time* (New York: The Free Press, 1999) p.113

off the ground to catch insects and land mammals becoming whales by wading in streams. These stories are a matter of opinion and aren't based on scientific evidence, which is why they change a lot.

For example, evolutionists think that whales evolved from small land mammals called *artiodactyls*. The hippo is their larger modern relative. However, they used to think that whales evolved from creatures called *mesonychids*. The story changed because molecular biologists discovered that hippos are the closest living relative of the whale.

Just-so stories are also used to explain why humans walk upright. Apparently, this happened because our ancestors lived in flooded areas and needed to keep their heads above water. Professor Chris Stringer of the Natural History Museum, London explains: 'I think that wading in a watery environment is as good an explanation, at the moment, for our upright gait as any other theory for human bipedalism.'*

Other evolutionists go a step further and believe that humans evolved from apes who lived in water. This theory explains why babies can swim when they're born. The sinuses (spaces in the skull behind the forehead) apparently helped the first humans float. We have large brains because of a chemical called docosahexaenoic acid that is found in fish. As Prof. Michael Crawford of Imperial College, London says: 'We got smart from eating fish and living in water.'**

All just-so stories have one big flaw. They can't explain how the story happened. It's just not scientific to say *why* something happens, evolutionists need to show *how* these physical changes occurred. None of these just-so stories can do this, so they're not proper science.

---

* R. McKie, Big brains, no fur, sinuses … are these clues to our ancestors' lives as 'aquatic apes'? *The Guardian* 27/04/2013. Retrieved from www.theguardian.com
** *Ibid*.

EVOLUTION AND ATHEISM

Believing in evolution is compulsory for biologists. Those that discover facts contradicting evolutionary theory usually end up in trouble. These people are respected scientists from well-known universities; they aren't creationists. For example, scientists who discovered the Trachilos footprints in Crete spent six years trying to get their results published because what they discovered didn't support evolutionary theory.

Scientists who are creationists find it even more difficult. In 2013 Mark Armitage from California State University announced that he had found soft tissue in a *Triceratops* fossil. Evolutionists didn't like this, because they find it hard to explain how fossils could have cells inside them after millions of years. Armitage was sacked for publishing his results even though they were scientifically correct. He was actually confronted by one professor who said: 'We are not going to tolerate your religion in this department.'* Armitage was awarded almost $400,000 for religious discrimination.

The theory of evolution is regularly weaponised by atheists and used to attack religion and belief in God. However hard they try, it's just not possible for evolutionary theory to disprove the existence of God.

THE ORTHODOX CHURCH AND EVOLUTION

In the Creed we confess that God is the maker of heaven and earth and of all things visible and invisible. We believe that God created all things out of non-being. We believe that our ancestors were Adam and Eve and that Christ is the Second Adam. We don't believe that man evolved from apes or any other life form. However, we're not creationists or evolutionists; we're Orthodox Christians.

The Old Testament book of Genesis, written by the Prophet Moses, contains the famous account of the creation of the

* www.insidehighered.com/news/2016/10/07/cal-state-northridge-settles-christian-lab-manager-who-said-he-was-fired-creationist

world. Remember though, that unlike the Gospels, the Creation account in Genesis wasn't written by an eyewitness. Moses didn't witness the Creation, but was inspired by the Holy Spirit to tell us about it.

Genesis is not just a history; it's a history revealed by God. In other words, we have to read Genesis in a deeper way than a history book. Some aspects of this account are hard to understand, which is why there is so much argument about evolution.

We believe in Creation, but most of the creationism that you will find on the Internet is Protestant and not Orthodox. Protestant Creationism is based on the idea that the Bible is more important than the Church. Reading Protestant books on Creation, therefore, isn't spiritually profitable for us, because they ignore the writings of the Orthodox Church Fathers. They also insist that everyone should understand the Bible literally like they do.

Others tend to ignore the literal meaning of the Bible. For these people, the Creation account is just symbolic. These Christian evolutionists are trying to make the Bible fit what science says at the moment.

Undoubtedly, there are many people in the Orthodox Church who believe in a 24 hour, six day creation. There's nothing wrong with this. On the other hand, there are plenty of Orthodox Christians who believe that the days before the creation of the sun might not have been 24 hours long.

We believe that God is the Creator and Sustainer of the world. It's not necessary for us to understand how He creates and sustains it. The only evolution we need to worry about is our spiritual evolution. Are we changing and growing in love for God and neighbour?

FREQUENTLY ASKED QUESTIONS

Was the world really created in six days?

Let's consider first of all the length of these six days. Were they actually 24 hours long? After all, the sun wasn't created until the fourth day. St. Basil the Great when discussing the first day of Creation says that the word 'eternity' expresses the same idea as 'day'.

St. Bede says that it's a mistake to try to work out the date of Creation by assuming all the first days of creation were 24 hours long. Talking about the making of the sun and moon on the fourth day, he said: 'During the first three days, as everyone can see, light and darkness weighed equally in the balance, for since the stars were not yet made, there was no measurement of hours.'*

On the other hand, other Fathers of the Church state that the days were 24 hours long. St. Ephraim the Syrian says that the day and the night of the first day were twelve hours long. To make sense of all this, we have to understand the writings of the Church Fathers in the context in which they were written.

Centuries ago people tried to calculate when the world would end by adding up the days since its creation. The Fathers pointed out that the first three days might not have been 24 hours long in order to stop these kind of calculations.

At the same time, there were people who taught that the world had always existed. The Fathers who taught a literal six day 24-hour Creation were trying to stop these people ignoring the Genesis account completely and thereby denying that God is the Creator of the world.

All the Fathers agree that the world was created as is described in the book of Genesis. Most of them have passed over the issue of how long it took because it's not particularly important.

---

* Venerable Bede *The Reckoning of Time* trans. F. Wallis (Liverpool: Liverpool University Press, 2004) p.24

What about the dinosaurs?

Evolutionists say that dinosaur fossils prove that the Creation account in Genesis is incorrect. They say that it's absolutely impossible for dinosaurs and humans to have lived together. On the other hand, people who believe in a literal six-day Creation (often referred to as 'young-earth creationists') say that the accounts of monsters and dragons in folk stories from around the world are evidence that humans met dinosaurs.

There are many drawings and cave paintings of animals which look like dinosaurs. Evolutionists are right, of course, when they say that not every 'dinosaur' cave painting is actually of a dinosaur. Sometimes, though, they are so worried about disproving them, they makes things worse! A group of archeologists decided that a group of cave paintings in Inner Mongolia were of giraffes and not dinosaurs. They forget, however, that according to evolutionary theory, giraffes became extinct millions of years before humans existed in this area.* Perhaps the giraffes painted self-portraits?

Everyone agrees that the Mokhali Cave paintings in Lesotho are of the *Ornithopod* dinosaur. These prehistoric cave paintings are scientifically more correct than the drawings that have been in textbooks for years. Evolutionists explain this by saying that these prehistoric scientists calculated what the dinosaur would look like from the fossilised tracks. Their belief in evolution doesn't let them consider the simpler explanation; the artist saw the dinosaur.

* R.G. Bednarik, Myths About Rock Art *Journal of Literature and Art Studies* August 2013, Vol. 3, No. 8, pp. 482-500

TRANSGENDER AND HOMOSEXUALITY

God created mankind as male and female, and we'll be judged in these bodies when we rise from the grave. In the Church, however, men and women are equal. St. Paul says that in the Orthodox Church 'there is neither Jew nor Greek, there is neither slave nor free, there is neither male nor female.' St. Basil the Great says that 'the virtue of man and woman is the same; creation is equally honoured in both, therefore there is the same reward for both.'

Men and women have different roles and responsibilities in Orthodoxy although they share the same reward. This reward is the Kingdom of Heaven which we can inherit by fighting against the passions.

This involves struggling against the sexual passions too. The Church will help us, but her teachings are clear. We believe in two genders, and that sexual intercourse outside marriage is sinful.

TRANSGENDER

Gender is something we are born with, not something that we choose. The Orthodox Church and traditional science agree completely about this. Our genes define our gender - not our personality.* Saying that someone can change gender through medical treatment isn't scientific and isn't Orthodox.

A man can never become a woman. Unfortunately, the biggest victims of the transgender movement are women. They're forced to share changing rooms and toilets with men. Women prisoners have been attacked in prison by male sex offenders identifying as women. Women's amateur sport is becoming meaningless as men are allowed to take part.

We're not saying though that boys must all like the same things. Some boys hate sport, but love reading books and playing musical instruments. Some girls love sport, climbing

* Some people are born with a physical intersex condition such as hermaphroditism. We are not talking about this here.

trees and playing with toy guns. These children aren't trapped in the wrong body. Likes and dislikes don't define gender.

People that believe that they have been born in the wrong body are suffering from a mental illness. Transgender activists say that hormone treatment followed by surgery can cure them. Treating the mentally ill like this is completely unacceptable to the Orthodox Church.

Unfortunately, the transgender movement is very powerful. They have managed to stop UK scientists researching into the growing problem of people regretting transgender surgery and wanting to change back again. Research carried out at John Hopkin's Hospital in America proves that many patients have the same thoughts after surgery as before. They still believe that they're in the wrong body. Surgery and hormone treatment mutilates, but it doesn't cure.

Because people who want to change gender are ill, we need to be careful what we say to them. They're mentally fragile and might be having suicidal thoughts. Speaking out against things like mixed toilets and changing rooms is fine. Confronting someone who is mentally ill isn't. We need to witness to Orthodoxy, but we must also lead people to the Church by our example of faith and love.

HOMOSEXUALITY

Wanting to change gender is a mental health problem; homosexuality, on the other hand, is a spiritual problem. The Orthodox Church has always said that having homosexual sex is a serious sin. The teaching of the Church is summarised by St. Paul in his letter to the Corinthians:

> Do not be mistaken: No fornicators, or idolaters, or adulterers, or effeminate persons, or those who sleep with men, or thieves, or lovers of money, or drunkards, or abusive talkers, or robbers, shall possess the kingdom of God.

However, we can see that homosexuality isn't singled out for special treatment; it's listed with many other sins which are just as destructive. All these sins, as St. John Cassian points out, are treated with the same remedy:

> There must be no doubt that the contagion of fornication and impurity can be done away with in our bodies, since he has commanded that they be cut off in the same way as love of money, foolishness, buffoonery, drunkenness, and thievery which are easily cut off.

St. Paul warned the Christians in Rome about the spiritual dangers of same-sex intercourse.

> For this cause God gave them up unto vile affections: for even their women did change the natural use into that which is against nature: And likewise also the men, leaving the natural use of the woman, burned in their lust one toward another; men with men working that which is unseemly, and receiving in themselves that recompense of their error which was meet.

St. John Chrysostom, commenting on these words of St. Paul, says that there's a difference between seeking out homosexual relationships and getting carried away due to ignorance or youth:

> This is why St. Paul did not say, being 'swept along' or being 'overtaken', expressions that he uses elsewhere, but instead he uses the word 'working'. They made a business of the sin and not only a business, but one eagerly entered into.

Youth doesn't excuse us from responsibility for these kinds of sins, but the Church understands that people make mistakes when they're young. Many young people go through a phase when they're confused about their sexuality.

Gay people are still cruelly bullied at school. Videos coming out of Russia show them being physically attacked in the street. These attackers are being tricked by the demons into hurting people in the name of Christ. We must set an example of Christian love and compassion, but without compromising our pure Orthodox faith.

We shouldn't participate in activities that promote homosexuality such as the Gay Pride events held in some schools. We shouldn't attend gay weddings or civil partnership ceremonies either.

FREQUENTLY ASKED QUESTIONS

If two gay people love each other why can't they marry?

We must not let physical love separate us from the love that Christ has for the Church. In Orthodox marriage a man and a woman are joined together as husband and wife. Their union is blessed by the Church, and this includes the union of sexual intercourse when the two become one flesh.

Marriage traditionally is between a man and a woman. The Church could never bless a relationship that involves sinful unnatural sexual acts such as anal or oral intercourse which take place between people of the same sex.

The Church rules don't just apply to gay people. Married couples that are having unnatural sexual intercourse and those who are having sexual intercourse outside marriage are not allowed to have Holy Communion.

Can gay people be cured?

Some Protestant churches and groups run courses for gay people with the aim of 'reprogramming' them. This is not how the Orthodox Church works. The Church is a spiritual hospital; all of us are spiritually ill.

Orthodox Christians don't refer to themselves as 'gay Orthodox' because being gay isn't something to be proud of; it's a cross we have to carry as best as we can. In the same way those of us troubled with other passions don't refer to ourselves as 'drink-too-much Orthodox' or 'angry Orthodox.' We should confess our sins in humility, but we shouldn't be proud or boast of them. Fr. Thomas Hopko sums this up brilliantly:

The tragic truth, however, is that countless people, especially in contemporary secularised societies, have *become convinced that their sinful thoughts and feelings, including, and even especially, those having to do with sex, are perfectly normal and natural and, as such, define who they are in their essential being and life. They therefore see no purpose or need in resisting, disciplining, and ultimately destroying them. They are convinced, on the contrary, that to do so would be dishonest, would be to deny and destroy themselves as persons, and, as such, would result in their personal death, which according to Christian Orthodoxy is the exact opposite of the truth.*[*]

So yes, gay people can fight against this passion, and they can overcome it. This is really hard work, but the grace of God helps and strengthens us, sometimes in a truly miraculous fashion. It might be that we still have feelings or thoughts that trouble us, but like all sinful thoughts we have to fight them with the weapons of prayer and fasting.

---

[*] T. Hopko, *Christian Faith And Same-Sex Attraction* (Ben Lomond: Conciliar Press, 2006) p. 35

ATHEISM

Atheism is the belief that there is no God. Most atheists aren't really atheists at all because they believe in some religious things but not others. For example, they believe in good and evil, which, as we shall see later, is impossible if you don't believe in God. Some believe in life after death. They refer to dead relatives as being 'at rest' or 'at peace'. A proper atheist would say that the dead simply cease to exist.

Most atheists we meet aren't really anti-Orthodox. They're just confused by the existence of so many different religions and beliefs that contradict each other.

The so-called 'New Atheists', on the other hand, are different. They mock religion and want to eliminate belief in God from all walks of life. They say that all religions are the same which is why they blame all religion for the bad things done by some religious people. This is obviously nonsense, but these views get a lot of media coverage so we will discuss them briefly.

ALL WARS ARE CAUSED BY RELIGION

Actually, most wars are about land and power, not religion. WW1 and WW2 started because Germany invaded neighbouring countries. They had nothing to do with religion.

The New Atheists often refer to the crusades when they blame religion for violence. The crusades, though, were nothing to do with Orthodoxy – they were a Roman Catholic idea. In fact, when the Fourth Crusade sacked Constantinople, thousands of Orthodox Christians were killed; for three days, the crusaders looted the city and defiled the holy places. On and off, for nearly three hundred years, popes organised crusades against Russian cities in order to convert them to Roman Catholicism.

Atheism isn't peaceful either. Communism killed at least 100 million people in the 20th century. Richard Dawkins says that he doesn't believe that there's an atheist in the world who would bulldoze Mecca, York Minster, or Notre Dame. History says different. Atheist Communist regimes destroyed hundreds of churches – not just with bulldozers but with explosives. The Cathedral of Christ the Saviour in Moscow (*right*) was blown up by the Communists in 1931.

Dawkins also says that 'individual atheists may do evil things but they don't do evil things in the name of atheism.'* History again says different. Communist regimes believed that violence and terror should be used to destroy religious belief. In 1930s Russia the prison sentence for just saying the 'Our Father' was ten years hard labour. Thousands of Orthodox clergy and lay people were killed because they were Christians. We commemorate all these New Martyrs who suffered under Communism on the Sunday nearest to 25 January.

VIOLENCE IN THE OLD TESTAMENT

New Atheists use the example of violence in the Old Testament to prove that God is not just or loving. Like today, people in the Old Testament who broke the law were punished. Some of the punishments might seem harsh to us, but this is because things were brutal back then. It wasn't until the early twentieth century that the world's most powerful countries agreed not to murder wounded enemy soldiers on the battlefield.

The Old Testament laws were for the Jews and their aim was to lead people to love of God and neighbour. Most of these

* R. Dawkins, *The God Delusion* (London, Bantam Press, 2006) p. 315-316

laws don't apply now. Even so, our society has adopted some of them. Murder is illegal, for example, because the Old Testament says so!

Finally, remember that those who died in the Old Testament heard the preaching of Christ in Hades. Even those punished by Old Testament law were granted to hear God's voice and accept His Word.

SUFFERING PROVES THAT GOD DOESN'T EXIST

Communism caused terrible suffering, but why does God allow the innocent to suffer? Why do people have to die in natural disasters and earthquakes?

We need to understand that even if earthquakes didn't exist, people would still die. The problem is not how we die, or how many we die with, but death itself. Christ however, has destroyed the power of death by His death on the Cross. We can now inherit eternal life with Him.

God cares for the world and sustains it. The care God has for the world is called providence. It's difficult for us to understand God's providence because our spiritual eyes are clouded by sins. If we start to doubt, we should call to mind these words of Saint Maximus the Confessor:

> It should not follow that, since the meaning of particular providence happens to be infinite and unknowable to us, we should make our ignorance a ground for denying the all-wise care for the things that are, but we should receive and hymn all the works of providence simply and without examination, as divinely fitting and suitable, and believe that what happens, happens well, even if the reason is beyond our grasp.[*]

There is something we can do about suffering. Earthquakes and disease tend to kill the poor because they don't have access to medicines or live in earthquake-proof buildings

---

[*] A. Louth, *Maximus the Confessor* (London: Routledge, 1996) p.147

like people in rich countries. God has given us free will so we can choose to help the poor, or not to help them.

We can choose to do something about suffering or to do nothing. God has given us free will because He loves us. If God was always stopping us from doing wrong we would soon start to hate Him for interfering. Think about how frustrated we feel when, as children, our parents force us to do things against our will, or stop us doing something that we want to do.

It's hard for us to make sense of suffering. However, each one of us can reduce the suffering of those around us by showing them love and compassion.

MORALS

Morals are our standards of behaviour - what we believe is right or wrong. The theological teachings of the Church are our morals. In the lives of the saints we read about how a truly moral life should be lived, because the saints believed morally and lived morally.

New Atheists don't believe in morals or even in good and evil. They believe that we are slaves to our DNA - we just do what it tells us to. Richard Dawkins, for example, says that morals evolved because society works better with them than without them. The following is an excerpt from an interview between Justin Brierley (JB) and Richard Dawkins (RD):

JB: If we'd evolved into a society where rape was considered fine, would that mean that rape is fine.

RD: I don't want to answer that question. It's enough for me to say that we live in a society where it's not considered fine.

JB: OK. But ultimately, your belief that rape is wrong is as arbitrary as the fact that we've evolved five fingers rather than six.

RD: You could say that, yeah.*

* J. Brierley, *Unbelievable?* (London: SPCK 2017) p.170-171

The New Atheists use the same argument when discussing Female Genital Mutilation (FGM). This procedure is illegal in the UK, which evolutionists would say makes us more evolved than African and Asian societies which carry it out. Orthodox Christians reject this racist idea. We condemn FGM because it's a sin. We don't say that societies that do it are less evolved than us – they're just doing something that is wrong.

THE CRUELTY OF ATHEISM

Extreme atheism doesn't have any morals – it's basically survival of the fittest. Atheistic Communist regimes encouraged parents to abandon their disabled children to be 'looked after' by the State. The conditions that these children lived in were terrible – especially for those who couldn't feed or wash themselves.

Nevertheless, there were people who were willing to help these children. They gave them food, washed them, comforted them and prayed with them. At Pascha they gave them paschal foods and dyed eggs. These people weren't educated atheists, but simple Orthodox Christians who risked everything to show love and compassion for strangers. One of these children says:

> Believing in God was forbidden. [The teachers] told us there was no God. I grew up where there was a fine line between life and death and meanness and nastiness were standard. There were very few caring attendants, full of kindness and concern. The good attendants believed in God. All of them. They believed no matter what.*

We have seen how brave Orthodox Christians cared for and brought joy and comfort to children abused by cruel atheism. During WW2 the Orthodox people of Zakynthos succeeded in hiding their Jewish neighbours to prevent them being sent to concentration camps. The bishop bravely

---

* R. Gallego, *White on Black* trans. M. Schwartz (London: John Murray, 2006) p. 26-27

told the German commander: 'If you choose to deport the Jews of Zakynthos, you must also take me, and I will share their fate.' When the island was hit by a powerful earthquake in 1953 the first boat to arrive with aid was from Israel, with a message that read: 'The Jews of Zakynthos have never forgotten their mayor or their beloved bishop and what they did for us.'*

FREQUENTLY ASKED QUESTIONS

Can atheists be good people?

Of course! The Holy Spirit is present everywhere and fills all things; when non-Orthodox people perform truly good actions they're opening their hearts to the Holy Spirit and allowing their conscience to act properly. We should learn from atheists that dedicate their lives to helping the poor and suffering. However, nothing is truly good except God. Our Christian life is not about becoming 'good' people, but through repentance, spiritual struggle and partaking of the Holy Mysteries to become gods by grace.

Why doesn't God destroy evil?

Evil entered the world because of the fall, which occurred first in the angelic kingdom and then on earth. Even though people do evil things, evil doesn't actually exist as a thing. It only appears when we choose it. Evil is a condition utterly opposed to the original condition in which we were created. God loves us so much, He has given us the gift of free will – to choose to reject or accept evil. The only way to remove evil from the world would be to remove all the people from it because we choose evil.

---

* http://www.ushmm.org/information/exhibitions/online-features/special-focus/holocaust-in-greece/zakynthos

READING LIST

All the following Orthodox books, magazines and websites are highly recommended. We should read as many of them as we can. The books are grouped according to publisher or distributor and are available from Orthodox bookstores.

ORTHODOX BOOKS

Centre for Traditionalist Orthodox Studies

Fr. James Thornton, *Seek Ye First the Kingdom*

Fr. James Thornton, *Delight in the Law of God*

Metropolitan Cyprian, *Do you have a ticket?*

Holy Transfiguration Monastery Translations

A Prayer Book for Orthodox Christians

The Pocket Psalter

Seraphim's Seraphim

Papa-Nicholas Planas

Saint Herman Press

Archimandrite Seraphim, *The Forgotten Medicine: The Meaning of Suffering, Strife and Reconciliation*

St. John Maximovitch, *The Orthodox Veneration of Mary the Birthgiver of God*

Blessed Theophylact, *Explanation of the Gospels*

Fr. Seraphim Rose, *God's Revelation to the Human Heart*

St. Theophan the Recluse, *Thoughts for Each Day of the Year*

Other Publishers

Fr. Steven Allen, *The Eternal Sacrifice: The Genesis Readings for Great Lent* (Lulu)

Alfredo Tradigo, *Icons and Saints of the Eastern Orthodox Church (Getty Publications)*

St. John Damascene, *The Precious Pearl (IBMGS)*

Archimandrite Joachim Spetsieris, *The Hermitess Photini* (St. Anthony's Greek Orthodox Monastery)

Barbara and Priscilla Johnson, *The Bread of Life A Collection of Orthodox Short Stories* (Saint Nektarios Press)

George Schaefer (trans.), *Living Without Hypocrisy: Spiritual Counsels of the Holy Elders of Optina* (Holy Trinity Monastery)

ORTHODOX CHRISTIAN MAGAZINES

Spiritual Watch www.hotca.org

Edification and Consolation www.hsir.org

ORTHODOX CHRISTIAN WEBSITES

www.orthodoxtruth.org

www.saintjohnsmonastery.org

www.thenunsgarden.org

FICTION

Jane Austen, *Pride and Prejudice*

John Buchan, *The Thirty-Nine Steps*

Wilkie Collins, *The Woman in White*

Charles Dickens, *Oliver Twist*

Arthur Conan Doyle, *The Adventures of Sherlock Holmes*

E.M. Forster, *A Room with a View*

C.S. Lewis, *The Space Trilogy*

Jack London, *The Call of the Wild*

Daphne Du Maurier, *Rebecca*

V.S. Naipul, *Miguel Street*

George Orwell, *1984*

George Simenon, *Maigret Goes to School*

Muriel Spark, *The Prime of Miss Jean Brodie*

Jonathan Swift, *Gulliver's Travels*

FICTION FOR YOUNG ADULTS

These books are not perfect, but they are better than the Young Adult fiction found on the shelves of school libraries. Those towards the end of the list are for older readers.

Antoine de Saint-Exupéry, *The Little Prince*

Louisa May Alcott, *Little Women*

Michael Morpurgo, *Private Peaceful*

Gary Schmidt, *Pay Attention, Carter Jones*

Kwame Alexander, *Booked*

John Anderson, *Posted*

Firoozeh Dumas, *It Ain't So Awful, Falafel*

J.R.R Tolkien, *The Hobbit* and *The Lord of the Rings Trilogy*

George Orwell, *Animal Farm*

Harper Lee, *To Kill a Mockingbird*

Maya Van Wagenen, *Popular: Vintage Wisdom for a Modern Geek*

Geraldine McCaughrean, *Where the World Ends*

S.E. Hinton, *The Outsiders*

William Golding, *Lord of the Flies*

Sophie Kinsella, *Finding Audrey*

POETRY

Selected Poems of Robert Frost: The Illustrated Edition

Phillip Larkin, *The Oxford Book of Twentieth Century English Verse*

NON-FICTION

James Herriot, *All Creatures Great and Small*

John Lennox, *God's Undertaker: Has Science Buried God?*

Jeffrey Burton Russell, *Exposing Myths about Christianity*

Walter Thomas, *Dare To Be Free*

Tim Severin, *The Brendan Voyage*

GLOSSARY

Aer: An embroidered cloth which is used to cover the chalice and diskos.

Altar: The area behind the iconostasis. Often also called the sanctuary.

Ambon: A Greek word meaning 'step'. The semi-circular area in front of the iconostasis where we receive Holy Communion.

Amen: A Hebrew word which means 'so be it' or 'this is right.'

Antidoron: A Greek word meaning 'instead of the gifts'. Antidoron is given to Orthodox Christians who have not received Holy Communion.

Antimension: (*See picture on p. 46*). The Divine Liturgy is served on the antimension and relics of martyrs are sewn into it.

Asterisk: (*See picture on p. 43*). Placed on the diskos to prevent the chalice veil from touching the Lamb. Represents the Star of Bethlehem.

Canons: The rulings of an Ecumenical or local Council.

Catechumen: Literally 'a hearer'. A person being taught the Orthodox Faith and preparing for baptism.

Censing: The offering of blessed incense to God. The incense is burned in a censer which is swung by the priest.

Chalice Veils: Cloths used to cover the chalice and diskos during the Liturgy.

Church Fathers: Saints of the Church who taught and wrote about the Orthodox Faith.

Consecration: The changing of the bread and wine into the Body and Blood of Christ during the Divine Liturgy.

Deification: Becoming gods by grace.

Diskos: (*See picture on p. 43*) A small metal plate on which particles cut from the prosphoron are placed.

Doctrine: The Orthodox beliefs taught by the Church.

Dismissal Hymn (Greek: *apolytikion*). A short hymn in honour of a saint or feast. Sung at the Little Entrance in the Liturgy.

Ecumenical Council: A gathering of bishops from all over the world that proclaims the Orthodox Faith.

Evangelist: The four writers of the Gospels: Matthew, Mark, Luke and John. Evangelist means 'Gospel-writer' in Greek.

Font: The water container used for baptism.

Fornication: Having sexual intercourse before marriage.

Frankincense: Grains of dried sap which produce a sweet smelling smoke when burned in the censer.

Gehenna: The place of everlasting torments that is prepared for sinners. Another name for hell.

Grace: The uncreated energies of God.

Heresy: Derived from the Greek verb 'to choose'. A belief that is different from Orthodoxy.

Hierarch: Literally 'High Priest' or 'Leader in holy things'. Another word for 'bishop'.

Holy Table: The table in the middle of the altar on which the Divine Liturgy is celebrated.

Horologion: Literally 'Book of Hours'. Contains the Daily Services of the Church.

Hypostasis: A Greek word meaning 'person' often used to refer to the Persons of the Trinity.

Incarnation: A word used to describe the Son of God taking on flesh and becoming man. From the Latin word *carnis* which means 'flesh'.

Iconostasis: The screen separating the sanctuary from the nave.

Jesus Prayer: Lord Jesus Christ, Son of God, have mercy on me, a sinner.

Kolyva: A dish of sweetened, boiled wheat prepared for blessing at memorial services.

Lamb: The central portion of the prosphoron cut out during the Service of Preparation. The Lamb becomes the Body of Christ.

Menaion: A set of twelve books containing the services of the saints for every day of the year.

Myrrh: A natural fragrant resin from trees.

Mystical: Having a hidden spiritual meaning. In a Mystery we see one thing and believe another.

Nameday: The saint's day or feast day after which we're named.

Narthex: The area at the back of the church separated from the nave by a partition.

Nave: The central part of the church.

Original Sin: Sometimes called the 'sin of Adam'. We inherit the consequences of this sin, but we are not guilty of it.

Octoechos: A Greek word meaning 'eight tones'. A book containing the text for the Sunday and weekday services in all the eight tones.

Pascha: The feast of the Resurrection of Christ. The word 'Pascha' comes from the Hebrew word for Passover.

Passover: The Hebrew Passover commemorates the passing of the angel over the houses of the Hebrews who had painted their door posts with the blood of the paschal lamb.

Passion: (1) From the Latin word for 'suffering'. The Passion of Christ describes His suffering and death on the Cross. (2) A passion is a sin that has become deeply rooted in us.

Pentecost: The descent of the Holy Spirit fifty days after Pascha.

Pentecostarion: A book containing the services from Pascha to Pentecost.

Polyeleos: Literally 'of much mercy'. The chandelier that is swung during the singing of Psalms 134 and 135. The word 'mercy' is repeated many times in these two psalms.

Prophets: These saints received the gift to foretell what was going to happen on earth and revealed the coming of Christ.

Proskomedia: Literally 'offering'. The Service of Preparation in which bread and wine are offered and prepared.

Prosphoron: (*See picture on p.42*). A round bread stamped with a special seal and used for the Divine Liturgy.

Prothesis Table: A table in the north-east corner of the sanctuary that is used in the Service of Preparation.

Repentance: A conscious decision to change our way of life by rejecting sin.

Righteous: People who keep the commandments of God. A title often given to Old Testament saints.

Righteousness: The act of performing our obligations to God by obeying His commandments.

Royal Doors: The doors in the middle of the iconostasis. These are more correctly called the Beautiful Gates.

Sabbath: The Hebrew word for Saturday.

Sanctuary: The area behind the iconostasis. Often called the 'altar'.

Sin: Literally 'missing the mark' or 'not making the grade'. A sin is something we do that falls short of Christ's commandments.

Temptation: Thoughts or desires that we have to resist in order not to fall into sin.

Theotokos: A Greek word meaning 'Mother of God'.

Triodion: A book containing the services of Great Lent.

Trisagion: The hymn 'Holy God, Holy Mighty, Holy Immortal have mercy on us.'

Unction: Literally 'anointing'. The oil sanctified in the mystery of unction is itself referred to as 'unction'.